Barking
From the Front Porch

by Gerald M. Sliva

◆ FriesenPress

Suite 300 - 990 Fort St

Victoria, BC, Canada, V8V 3K2

www.friesenpress.com

Edited by Cecilia Sliva and Barbara Berscheid

ISBN

978-1-4602-6981-7 (Hardcover)

978-1-4602-6982-4 (Paperback)

978-1-4602-6983-1 (eBook)

1. *Biography & Autobiography, Personal Memoirs*

Distributed to the trade by The Ingram Book Company

Contents

Part Two
Kuroki, Buckhorn Bay and Beyond

Part Three
Recipes

Part Four
Appreciation and Invitation

Families are like fudge — mostly sweet with a few nuts.

This book is dedicated to all families, large and small, each with their own blessings and trials, joys and sorrows. Special mention must go to my own families – my ancestors who braved the unknown to settle in Canada, the family into which I was born, the family into which I married, the family I formed together with Cecilia, and the family of our son, daughter-in-law and precious granddaughter.

May it also be a remembrance to all children who died before their time and to the grieving mothers who bore them.

You are all treasures to me.

Part One
Kuroki Days

Good Morning

Dawn breaks and the world awakes
to breakfast in the clouds.
Orange sun and apricot skies
God's giant juicer liquefies.
Dawn breaks and the world awakes
to drink in the view ~
Our Creator making nectar
before our very eyes.
Fresh squeezed juices ~ King size!

*God will be present, whether asked
or not. - Latin Proverb*

Prologue

We know the worth of a thing when we have lost it. – French Proverb

November 12, 2014

My Dear Alicia,

You really don't know me, but I'm your Dad and Cecilia is your Mother. As you listen to my stories you will get to know us better. Also, I'll introduce you to a lot of other relatives and friends as time goes on, but right now I'd like to concentrate on why I'm writing to you – it's your brother's fault, and I'll explain why. For a couple years now I've been trying to write a book, and I really didn't know the reason why. Your Mother and a few other relatives have been reading a little of what

I wrote and commenting on it, but then your brother, Greg – he's an intelligent, handsome fellow just like his Dad – spent one evening scanning what I had written. He liked my writing style, my sense of humour, and he found my stories interesting, BUT! Those "but's" always get in the way of making us happy; that's part of life. Greg went on to suggest that I might make the whole book more interesting if I could somehow tie all my stories together, maybe by writing directly to someone. Great idea, Greg! But now I've got to rethink my approach. That's hard work! Anyways, I thought about his critique very seriously for many hours. To whom was I going to write? Who might want to hear my story? I didn't know, but I went to bed to let it sink in. Then at three o'clock this morning you woke me up and asked me to tell you about life.

Immediately, I pictured you, Alicia, my pretty little daughter sitting on my knee and saying to me, "Daddy, tell me about life."

And I replied to you, "I would love to do that, Alicia, but it will take some time. Life is a little complicated, full of heartache, loads of fun and many mysteries. I'll do my best. Thank you for asking me."

I don't want this to get boring for you, so I'll try to tell you some humorous, some sad and some nostalgic incidents about some of your ancestors, my growing up as a young boy, and my life with my son - your brother – Greg, and my wife - your Mother - Cecilia. It will be hard to know where to start, but before I get too far into my stories you'll notice that I love food. The whole Sliva clan enjoys their food and drink so much that I think that food and drink are somehow fondly mentioned in about eighty percent of what I've written. With that in mind I've thrown in a few specific comments on food and drink as well as some of my favorite traditional family recipes, all of which you would love. Daddies are supposed to give advice too, so I've included a little of that.

My granddaughter, Robyn, knows how much I love sayings, proverbs and witty quotations, so as part of each little story about life I have included a proverb – some of them are as old as the pyramids, and some that I've made up are as new as this morning's sunrise.

Life is a mystery, Alicia, sometimes sad but sometimes loads of fun. To start with here's a whimsical little story about God's creation of life – it's an old story, so I hope you haven't heard it before.

> On the first day, God created the dog and said, "Sit all day by the door of your house and bark at anyone who comes in or walks past. For this I will give you a life span of twenty years." The dog said, "That's a long time to be barking. How about giving me only ten years and I'll give you back the other ten?"

> God agreed. And God said that it was good.

> On the second day, God created the monkey and said, "Entertain people, do tricks, and make them laugh. For this, I'll give you a twenty-year life span."

The monkey said, "Monkey tricks for twenty years? That's a pretty long time to perform. How about I give you back ten like the dog did?"

And God again said that it was good.

On the third day, God created the cow and said, "You must go into the field with the farmer all day long and suffer under the hot sun, have calves and give milk to support the farmer's family. For this, I will give you a life span of sixty years."

The cow said, "That's kind of a tough life you want me to live for sixty years. How about making it twenty and I'll give back the other forty?"

God agreed and it was good.

On the fourth day, God created humans and said, "Eat, sleep, play, marry and enjoy your life. For this, I'll give you twenty years."

But the human said, "Only twenty years? Could you possibly give me the twenty you already offered, the forty the cow gave back, the ten the monkey gave back, and the ten the dog gave back; that makes eighty, okay?"

"Okay," said God, "You asked for it."

So that is why for our first twenty years, we eat, sleep, play and enjoy ourselves. For the next forty years, we slave in the sun to support our family. For the next ten years, we do monkey tricks

to entertain the grandchildren. And for the last ten years, we
sit on the front porch and bark at everyone.

— Source Unknown

So, Alicia, I'm getting a little older now. Life has been entertaining to say the least. The last ten years I've tried to do monkey tricks to entertain our granddaughter, Robyn, and it has been such a pile of fun. But, if eighty years is really the life span we are destined to get, I am in the "barking" stage of my life.

I'm no Biblical scholar, but to determine the veracity of this account of God's creation of animals and mankind I combed through both the old and new testaments and found no such evidence. However, I did find one main theme: Love God and love your neighbour. Somewhere else in the Bible I heard Jesus say, "Go ye and do likewise!"

Alicia, that's nearly the end of the story; I could stop my story about life right there; I've told it all; life is about love or at least it should be. But you say you want to hear the beginning and the middle too. I love you, and I hope you will find lots of love in my story about life, but first I need to tell you about your own very short life. Sadly we never had a chance to hold you and to tell you we love you. Your life started and ended hooked up to all sorts of instruments in an incubator at St. Paul's Hospital in Saskatoon, Saskatchewan in the space of just forty hours in 1967. You were three months premature, and your tiny lungs just could not hold enough air to sustain life in your fragile little body. We said good-bye way too soon.

That happened forty-seven years ago, and now I'm getting to be an old dog. Sometimes I bark; sometimes I wag my tail at neighbours and friends; sometimes I growl when I see Pharisees and politicians; sometimes I chase cars, and sometimes I just lie on the rug in front of the fireplace and dream, snore and pass gas.

I'll start barking now, Alicia. I have experienced life, and I will try to share it with you.

I love you, and I thank you for asking me to share my story.

Love,

Dad

P.S. All the stories are for you, Alicia, but I want to tell my story to the whole world as well, so rather than using my handwriting, I'll switch to an easier to read font. When I am speaking mainly to you, Alicia, I will use my own handwriting.

My life started in Regina, Saskatchewan at the Grey Nuns Hospital on February 2, 1944. I was born on Groundhog Day! Sometimes I'm teased about that, but it's great to have a birthday that people remember while I compete for the limelight with Wiarton Willie in Canada and Punxsutawney Phil in the U.S.A. - each of us trying to predict the weather. I'll make my beginnings a really short story, because I don't remember any of it except for the stories my dad and mom told me as well as from the stories told by the old family photos I have in my possession.

When I was born the Second World War was in progress. My dad, Mike Sliva was posted as Staff Sergeant at the Military hospital in Regina, Saskatchewan, and my mother, Anne Sliva worked in a munitions factory in Regina assembling big guns to help defeat the Nazis and to liberate Europe from a mean fellow named Hitler. After the war my dad tried a short stint at farming in the Dobrowody district of Saskatchewan - I'll tell you more about that later - then he decided he wanted to be a big businessman, so in 1949 he bought the Kuroki Hotel in partnership with my mom's brother, Mike Mazer. I was just about five years old at the time, and that's the part of my life when I really started to remember things, so that's where I can start telling you about life - at least about my life.

Generic Kuroki*

Home is a place you grow up wanting to leave, and grow old wanting to get back to. - John Ed Pearce

Kuroki was my home town. You might not know it, but anyone who grew up anywhere in North America in the 1950's grew up in Kuroki, Saskatchewan or in the rural area nearby. Kuroki was home. Maybe your "Kuroki" was different from mine, but for you it was home. Maybe it was in Saskatchewan, but it could have been in Alberta or Ontario, even New York or California. Growing up in the 50's meant you grew up in a neighbourhood. You played with friends out on the streets; you said "Hello" to everyone you met, and you addressed as "Mr." or "Mrs." anyone who was twenty years older than you or who was married.

Wherever your "Kuroki" was you knew everyone, and everyone knew you, and everyone was your friend – a lot like the *Cheers* bar in the old TV sitcom.

Back in the late 1940's and 1950's my Kuroki was a vibrant little town with a Post Office, a hotel (my dad's hotel), three grain elevators, a lumber yard, a John Deere farm implement dealer, a Massey Harris implement dealer, a couple auto repair shops, a blacksmith shop, a two room red brick school, a livery stable, two shoe repair shops, Kanigan's Café, a couple general stores, the Coop store, a municipal office for the Rural Municipality of Sasman, four churches, a curling rink, skating rink and a dance hall. Everyone had a huge garden. People hadn't yet heard the term "organic gardening". They just practiced it.

If you grew up in a slightly larger "Kuroki" you might have had a cooperative creamery, a bank or credit union, a barber shop, a beauty parlour, a movie theatre, a drive-in theatre, a hardware store, a women's dress store, a photo studio, a pool hall, a pharmacy where you could buy Superman, Batman, Lone Ranger and Archie comics for a dime each, a doctor, a dentist and maybe even a hospital.

In my Kuroki a CNR passenger train chugged through town twice each day dropping off people, full beer kegs, groceries, empty cream cans and mail, then picking up people, empty beer kegs, full cream cans and mail. Twice each day during the summer kids, either walking, running or riding bicycles, hurried to beat the passenger train to the station, placing pennies on the tracks hoping they wouldn't bounce off before the 350 ton steam locomotive flattened them into shiny souvenirs. If they were young enough, they even had discussions about not putting too many pennies on the track for fear of derailing the train. When the train finally pulled into the station, they watched wide-eyed as the Negro porters helped passengers disembark and still others begin their journey to who-knows-what exotic places like Saskatoon or Winnipeg, Toronto or Vancouver. There was a beehive of activity as the steamer disgorged its contents and picked up more; within minutes the conductor shouted "All aboard" as the steamer hissed, smoked and puffed. The engineer gave two quick toots of the whistle, and the train hurried off to the next town on its route. Then when the train left the station, the children would scurry around trying to find their flattened penny souvenirs.

On Saturday night the streets were lined with vehicles of every description, and the beer flowed freely in the smoke filled "males only" beer parlour with beer at 10 cents a glass. At nine p.m. the local band started playing at Kuroki Hall where most of the wives and girlfriends visited or danced with each other until the beer parlour closed at 11:00 p.m. and the men had consumed sufficient quantities of beer to make them believe that they were terrific dancers.

On Sunday morning most people dressed up in their fancy duds and went to church where the ladies put on a huge lunch after the service, the men stood around smoking and discussing the weather, the crops and the newest John Deere tractors being offered for sale while the children visited and played tag around the spruce trees in the churchyard.

It was a simpler time and a fun time. Pregnant women were a common sight. There were larger families with five to eight kids or more. But not everyone could take over the family farm. Students graduated from school, went on to jobs in the big city or to study at University to become teachers, nurses, doctors, lawyers and engineers. They couldn't practise their chosen profession in "Kuroki", so they moved to the big city – Saskatoon, Calgary, Toronto or even New York - leaving their fathers to die, creating many a ghost town except for their widow mothers and the odd retired farm couple who couldn't afford to move to a larger town or the big city.

The offspring of "Kuroki" now populate three quarters of Ontario and fifty percent of British Columbia as well as filling the three Prairie Provinces.

There is nothing generic about your "Kuroki" or mine. There was, and still is, pride in the old home town. It was a lot like "Rider Pride" or cheering for the Bombers, Marauders or Wildcats, whatever the home team was called. It was a great place to grow up, and we might still live in "Kuroki" if there were jobs for us and for our families. It was and still is home.

*Kuroki (pronounced: koo-roh-key) is a pretty little hamlet situated about three hundred kilometres East of Saskatoon along the Canadian National rail line in the province of Saskatchewan. In the 1950's the population of Kuroki was about 150 people plus numerous dogs and cats. It was named after the Japanese general Kuroki Tamamoto. During the Russo-Japanese War of 1904 and 1905 Japan and Britain were allies against Russia. Japanese names and traditions became quite popular among the British. Two other towns, Mikado and Togo, along the CN line in Saskatchewan were also named in honour of the Japanese.

Billboard at western edge of hamlet of Kuroki

A Lovely Bottle of Orange Crush

Family is the glue that holds the fabric of society together — sometimes it's crazy glue.

I started with my home town, Alicia, but life isn't only about "home town"; it's about family, doing things with each other, for each other and about love. It's also about extended family, about relatives.

Everyone should have a favourite uncle. My mother with five siblings and my father with six, grew up in large families, and I was blessed with having many favorite uncles and aunts. I give thanks for all of them.

It was hard to choose the best among them. They were all the chosen ones at one time or another.

But everyone should have an Uncle Joe who owns a farm. I did. He was my dad's brother, just a few years older than Dad. My first remembrances of him were from the early 1950's. He was a sociable, friendly sort of fellow who always had a smile on his face, making his nephews feel at home with his gentle teasing. He had time for us, frequently smoking and joking while showing us the ways of the farmer, the farm machinery and the farm animals. He lived on a small farm, in a small house about an hour's drive on dusty dirt roads from where we lived in the tiny hamlet of Kuroki, Saskatchewan. Every visit with Uncle Joe and Aunt Zonie was an adventure, particularly when my brother Don and I were in the pre-teen relatively innocent times of our lives.

It was the early 1950's, the days before refrigeration and electricity in rural Saskatchewan. When we visited on the farm we saw ice houses (not houses made of ice, but houses used to store ice all summer long) and deep, cold wells used for refrigeration. Cows were milked by hand. There were horses, sheep, ducks and chickens. We helped hand-crank the cream separator and the butter churn. The gardens were huge and the food was terrific. We ate fresh vegetables, hand-made perogies, fresh dill pickles with lots of garlic, unforgettably delicious home canned chicken preserved in large two-quart glass sealers, thick slices of fresh home baked bread dripping with gobs of home churned butter and awesome juicy fresh picked strawberries with warm, freshly separated sweet cream for dessert. It was simple fare, loads of it, and we ate like kings!

On one particular beautifully warm Sunday morning in June, 1953 my mother, dad, my brother Don, our little sister Barbara and I were making the trek to Uncle Joe's farm. I was nine, Don was seven and Barb was two.

Life was great! We three kids were in the back seat of Dad's 1950 two door grey Chevy. Mom and Dad had loaded us down with Orange Crush and bags of chips to keep us quiet until we reached our destination. Our interim destination was the Saints Peter and Paul Roman Catholic Church in the Dobrowody (Polish meaning "good water") district about seven miles north-east of Rama, Saskatchewan. The church was only four miles from Uncle Joe's farm. It was a rural parish where we had planned to meet Uncle Joe and his family, attend Sunday Mass with them, and then travel together to the farm for a day of relaxation, adventure, shenanigans and major feasting.

It turned out that Mom and Dad's plans to keep us entertained with pop and chips in the back seat were ill conceived. There were no seat belts to keep us restrained in a 1950 Chevy, so Don and I found ways to pester each other by poking, prodding and generally harassing one another with Dad periodically threatening to stop the car and give us something to think about. Before long, however, the two bottles of Orange Crush I had consumed were having an effect on my bladder causing me to begin pleading with Dad to stop the car because I had to pee. It was to no avail. Dad was focused on getting to church on time and kept telling me that it was only ten minutes more, or seven minutes more, or four minutes more and I could wait until we got to the church. There was an outhouse in the churchyard where he said I could relieve myself. He said I should just sit quiet and wait! That's easy for an adult to say, but difficult for a nine year old to do. Every few minutes I would protest that I really had to go, and Dad kept retorting that there were only a few more miles to go and that I could wait. Finally I said that if he didn't stop I would pee my pants.

In exasperation, just two miles from the church, he said, "Just pee in one of the empty pop bottles back there."

Well, I didn't need to be told that more than once. I felt my bladder ready to explode. Unzipping my fly and grabbing an empty Orange Crush bottle, I filled it to the top within a few seconds with nice warm yellow pee, but once I started I couldn't stop. Asking Don to take the bottle I had filled and to spill it out the window - two bad ideas, but what does a nine year-old know? - I quickly grabbed another empty and was proceeding to fill that when suddenly Don, upon feeling the warm bottle and smelling the ammonia of the pee I had handed him, began a violent retching and threw up all over the back seat of our nice Chevy. As quickly as he could, Dad slammed on the brakes skidding to a dusty, gravel-flying halt, but not before two year old Barbara got a whiff of Don's vomit and let loose with her own explosion of puke.

It was a sight to behold: all of us dressed in our Sunday best, stumbling from the car, dust and barf flying everywhere, Don and Barb continuing to vomit, the rest of us gagging from the smell, Dad muttering words under his breath that weren't really prayers on that Sunday morning while Mom tried to clean things up as best she could.

The upshot of it all was that we made it to church about fifteen minutes after the Mass had begun, but we still had time to sit down, pray and ask forgiveness for all our sins of the previous half hour.

As we reflect back on the journey to church and Uncle Joe's farm that beautiful spring day in 1953, we may be thankful for the lessons we learned on that occasion.

First lesson: There is nothing to be gained by reminding Dad that it was his idea that I pee in the bottle.

Second lesson: Sometimes you can save time, energy and frustration by stopping when your passengers say they need a bathroom break.

Third lesson: Although Uncle Joe's farm is a great place to visit, sometimes the adventure is not in the destination but rather in the journey. It certainly was on that day.

Fourth lesson: Some of the most ridiculous situations and the most annoying occurrences provide the best fodder for family reminiscences, especially when embellished somewhat and more especially when they occurred in the distant past rather than just a few minutes ago.

Where do Chickens Come From?

He who pursues an innocent chicken always stumbles. - Nigerian Proverb

As I mentioned, Alicia, there were vegetables, fruits, cattle, sheep, ducks and chickens on Uncle Joe's farm.

We knew all these things were raised as food. We knew they came from the farm. In contrast, life can be far too innocent for many children in modern North American society. They are unaware of the blood and the gore associated with the meats that we eat. They have access to all the information and misinformation available on the internet, yet they can have little realization of how the basic necessities of life are produced. In the larger metropolitan areas, particularly in the downtown core of the city, many children almost never see a garden, hog or chicken pen, or any cattle except perhaps in magazine photographs or colouring books. In contrast, most youngsters growing up prior to 1950 knew exactly where fruits, vegetables and pork, beef and chicken came from. There were gardens in almost every back yard as well as cows, pigs, chickens, goats and sheep either right in town or just on the edge of it.

In the early 1950's most small towns and farms in Saskatchewan were just beginning to receive the benefits of an electrical power grid. Many families still used coal oil lamps or gas lamps for lighting and had little or no access to refrigerators and freezers for preserving food. Home canning of berries, fruits and vegetables was common. Meat had to be canned or kept in rented commercial freezer space called a locker plant, available in some of the larger towns. Many households both on farms and in towns kept chickens in small pens in their back yards as a source of fresh meat.

In the tiny hamlet of Kuroki, in the back yard behind my dad's hotel, we kept such a chicken pen. My parents would occasionally purchase eight or ten chickens from a local farmer, keep them until needed, butcher one or two for fresh meat, then feed and water the remainder until it was time for them to become tonight's roast chicken and tomorrow's home-made chicken soup. It was the way things were done, and although I participated in the dining, I did not participate in the harvesting of the hens until one fateful late September day in 1955.

I was eleven years old, and Mom determined that it was time for me to play a part in the collecting of the chickens for that evening meal. She gave me a hefty butcher knife, which to an innocent eleven year old, appeared to be no less than four feet long and twenty pounds in weight. She hurriedly instructed me on the procedure to follow: how to catch the chicken, hold it firmly yet gently, how to stroke its head and calm it, how to lay its neck on the chopping block, and then how to execute (pun intended) the ghastly chore. I tried to get out of it by telling Mom I had to go out and play "Cowboys and Indians" - we weren't too politically correct back then. Mom would have none of that, and she insisted that I was to select one chicken and to invite it to the dinner table. I had watched my dad perform the gruesome task on several occasions, and along with my brother had giggled at how the chickens hopped and sometimes ran about after their heads were severed, blood squirting in every direction. We knew the true meaning of the saying, "running around like a chicken with its head cut off", but we didn't really give it a second thought.

But now it was my turn to do the dirty deed. This was not going to be easy. Not having previously committed premeditated murder, I was extremely apprehensive. I knew what was expected of me, and I tried to be brave, but my heart was shuddering inside. Warily and reluctantly, trudging to the chicken pen at the back of our property, I lay the murder weapon alongside the chopping block for easy access when I needed it. Then opening the gate, entering the pen and closing the gate behind me, I slowly stalked my quarry hoping to find an easy prey. I dreaded the task, and every last one of the birds must have sensed my trepidation, for they all avoided my efforts to coax them into my lethal grip. After some minutes of talking to them in what I thought was a soothing voice, I finally coaxed one into these treacherous arms. Holding it like a puppy, I stroked it until it seemed to be calm, then with one hand I opened the gate, closed it behind me and carried my victim to the guillotine. As I approached the chopping block I covered the chicken's eyes with one hand and stroked it gently with the other as I held it in my lap. The butcher knife was where I had laid it, so with one quivering hand I reached for the murder weapon while cradling the bird close to me with the other. I had no clear plan and wondered how I would hold the knife, calm the chicken and lay its neck on the chopping block all at the same time. I needed one more hand. Finally it occurred to me that I had to put the knife down, sooth my victim by stroking its head with one hand while holding it gently with the other and slowly moving its neck over the wood stump we used as a chopping block. Then when the neck was stretched out and the time seemed right, I nervously reached for the knife and with one motion closed my eyes, swung the deadly weapon and let go of the chicken. I heard a blood curdling squawk and opened my eyes to see the chicken running in circles and bleeding profusely. The next few minutes were a blur as feathers, dust and blood flew everywhere. Through my tear-filled eyes I saw that I had given my quarry only a glancing blow, cutting off part of its comb, a portion of its head, one eye and the complete beak. Chaos reigned. I was terrified, but I knew exactly what to do next – PANIC! I did so, dropping the knife and breaking into uncontrollable sobs.

Fortunately for me and unfortunately for the chicken, my dad must have been watching my amateur efforts through the kitchen window, and at that point decided to come to my rescue. After a little scurrying around chasing the now quite agitated, uncooperative and seriously injured chicken, Dad captured the prey and made quick work of what had taken me so long to mess up. I must have made a good impression that day, for never again was I asked to be the butcher. It was many months before I could again eat chicken without reliving that horrid scene in my mind. But the trauma recovery must have been rapid. We had chicken stew for supper that night, and I ate my fill. I do not recall ever having refused to eat chicken; I have not resorted to vegetarianism, and to this day I relish the thought of stuffed roast chicken and gravy, providing I am not the one expected to euthanize the feathery creatures.

Cool, Clear Water

*You never miss the water till the well
has run dry. – Irish Proverb*

In 1953 Uncle Joe's farm was loads of fun, but by today's standards it would have been considered primitive. For instance, there was no such thing as electricity or running water. Water is the source of all life. It is such a precious resource, but we now take it for granted. We turn one tap to get cold drinking water; we turn another tap to get hot bathing water. We use as much as we want, when we want and think nothing of it. But we're not happy with what comes from our taps. We want bottled drinking water. We will pay one or two dollars for a small bottle of Aquafina or some generic brand of drinking water and think we are getting a bargain. Some marketing genius has convinced us that if he takes water out of some tap, puts it in a fancy looking plastic bottle with a snow-capped mountain on the label we will be dumb enough to pay for it. He is right! When I grew up, our friends would have called us idiots if we paid money for bottled water; in fact it wasn't available even if we wanted to buy it. Our experiences with water were different in the "olden" days.

In my early childhood the securing and use of water was similar to what still occurs in some Third World countries. It was used sparingly because it was time consuming to obtain as well as to dispose of after it was dirty. Before 1955 very few people in small towns or on farms had running water. Families spent many hours securing sources of water for washing, drinking and cooking. Such was the case in Kuroki.

One block south of our hotel, for the use of all townspeople, there was a deep municipal well, a hand operated pump and a dugout. Each day we carried water in galvanized steel pails from the well to our hotel for drinking and cooking purposes. The water from the municipal well was great drinking water - cold, clear and delicious - with rarely a need for chlorination. Besides, it was free! One of the fun things when we were growing up was playing cricket using old Texaco oil cans as wickets on hot summer days, working up a huge thirst, then heading for the municipal pump to take turns pumping while others took turns cupping their hands under the spout and quenching themselves

with the coldest, most refreshing beverage known
to mankind. When I think back, it is probably fifty-
five years since I had a drink of truly delicious water,
nothing at all like the tasteless stuff that various com-
panies now try to sell in plastic bottles for outrageous
sums of money. Depending on the number of guests
staying over in our hotel we often needed to make
several trips a day to that municipal well to replenish
the drinking water supply. Even at the tender age of
ten I was helping to haul the water even though I could
carry only a half pail in each hand. The water was terrific for drinking but it was "hard" water and not really
the best for washing. In any event, it would have been
an onerous task to carry sufficient water from the well
for cleaning and washing floors, clothing, bedding,
dishes, our faces and hands as well as for our baths.

The water for these cleaning tasks often came from
cisterns just under the kitchen floor of most homes as
well as our hotel. These cisterns were huge concrete
storage tanks which held from 5,000 to 10,000 gallons
of rainwater collected off the roofs when it rained.
When it didn't rain for long periods of time, water had
to be hauled in from dugouts or sloughs to replenish
the cistern. During the winter when the cistern water
would sometimes run low, I remember my dad opening
the trap door to the cistern and spending many hours
shovelling snow into the cistern. There, the snow
would melt and provide us with more water. In the

kitchen there was a small hand pump for bringing the water up from the cistern for use primarily in washing clothes, taking baths or for washing our hands and face. The cistern water, being primarily rainwater was not suitable for drinking, but it was "softer" water with fewer dissolved minerals and was better for the washing chores. So we pumped the water up from the cistern and filled a pitcher which we kept near a wash basin on a wash stand in one corner of the kitchen for washing our hands and faces. Under the wash stand there was a slop pail for discarding dirty water after we washed. Then, when the slop pail was full we hauled it outside and dumped it in the outhouse. So, if it was such a production just to wash our hands and faces you can imagine what the once-a-week bath night was like.

Yep, we had a bath only once a week, and it was a huge undertaking involving many hours of labour. First, we pumped water up from the cistern, heated it on the wood-fired kitchen stove and poured it into the bathtub. There was often only one or two inches of water at the bottom of the tub, and the same water was used for almost all family members to bathe in, with just a little more hot water added for each new bather and then a little more warm water for rinsing the body and hair. When everyone had finished their baths you couldn't just pull the plug and let the dirty water drain away. There was no sewer system. Every drop of dirty water had to be poured out of the tub, into a slop pail and hauled outside to be dumped into the ditch, garden or the outhouse. We might have wanted to bathe more than once a week, but the whole event took so much time and energy that it was a real effort to accomplish it even once a week. One of the luxuries we now expect and take for granted is a daily shower or bath. It didn't happen in Kuroki or any other small town. In 1950 when people called us dirty little buggers they were just stating a fact.

In about 1953 Dad had a well dug in our back yard, had a pump attached to it and had a plumber install pipes for running water and flush toilets in the hotel. Pure luxury! But all was not perfect. Since there was no sewer system in town Dad had to have a septic tank and a cesspool installed near the hotel. The septic tank kept plugging up, and the cesspool, even though it was gigantic, had to be pumped out once or twice a year and taken to the landfill for disposal. Another problem was that we had only cold running water. We couldn't afford a water heater large enough for the hotel. Then one more problem: after the water was tested by the Department of Health we were advised that it was bacteria free, could be used for cooking and washing, but that it contained excessive sulfates and should not be regularly consumed by children under the age of three. To be on the safe side we used the water from our taps only for washing and cooking. We continued our daily treks to the municipal pump for our drinking water until 1962 when Dad sold the hotel, then renovated and added on to the post office building into which we moved. There, he had another well dug, and we had the luxury of hot and cold running water. We were finally part of civilized twentieth century society rather than members of the great unwashed!

Your Sweet Biffy

*I have this terrible disease:
everything I eat turns to poop!*

*Alicia, believe it or not, before 1953, with no running water
we certainly didn't have flush toilets either.*

Under most beds there was a Chamber pot (we called it
a potty) which we used if we had to go to the bathroom
during the night. Sometimes when we were really sleepy
we missed the pot, spraying urine all over the floor and
stepping on it when we got up in the morning. Besides
the potty, we stored other items under the bed. One
Christmas my parents had bought me a brown suede
cowboy suit complete with a vest and chaps. I loved that
cowboy suit, used it frequently for playing "Cowboys

and Indians", and stored it in a corrugated cardboard box under our bed - my brother Don and I slept in the same bed. One night while in a deep sleep I got up to pee, couldn't find the potty, pulled out the box containing my cowboy suit and gave it a real soaking. I was so tired that I didn't realize what had happened until the next morning. You can imagine how much teasing I got about that episode. We had to throw out the cardboard box, and Mom washed my cowboy suit, but being of imitation leather it really didn't look authentic after the urine bath I gave it. I never wore it again.

Each morning we had to haul the smelly potty to the outhouse to discard the contents. Sometimes when we were younger we tended to be rather lazy and didn't dump the pot out each morning. As you can imagine, the potty got close to overflowing and our bedroom got rather stinky after several days. It seems that eight and nine year old boys are quite tolerant of strong urine smells - unless it is fresh urine in pop bottles in the back seat of a gray 1950 Chevy. Before 1953, since we had no flush toilets, if we had to pee or poop during the day we went to an outdoor toilet – a little house on the prairie.

Those of us who grew up in the 1940's and 1950's and earlier in small prairie towns or on farms regularly visited a little house on the prairie. This building was a compact one or two-hole structure, although some larger towns like Steinbach, Manitoba sported out-buildings which accommodated six or eight people simultaneously at the rear of their large school and church – communal urination and defecation at its finest! The said structure was to be found in the back yard of all small town residences some sixty to ninety feet from the back door of each house as well as behind most churches, schools, stores and public offices. These little houses on the prairie were variously referred to as toilets, biffies, crappers, shitters, shit houses, crap cans, backhouses, or outhouses.

Many were never painted or decorated except for the traditional crescent moon sometimes cut into the door. Some received an occasional coat of poor quality leftover white, brown or red barn paint, and still others were given an occasional coat of whitewash and thusly named "The White House" where folks would go to "visit Eisenhower" (Dwight Eisenhower was the President of the United States back then.) My old Uncle Walter whitewashed his outhouse regularly, keeping its exterior looking quite white and spotless compared to the many weathered, dilapidated out-buildings in the rest of town. His eldest son purchased an "OFFICE" sign and nailed it to the door of that old whitewashed building prompting Uncle Walter to regularly announce that he was going to the office to do some paper work, and that he didn't want to be disturbed. His outhouse became a local tourist attraction.

Speaking of paper work, commercially produced ass wipe was an expensive and somewhat scarce commodity in the mid twentieth century. Most outhouses kept an ample supply of old newspapers, last year's Eaton's and Simpsons-Sears catalogues or the wrappings from what were known as "Jap" Oranges – very politically incorrect – they were Japanese Mandarin Oranges which were a special Christmas treat each year. Needless to say, these makeshift toilet papers were usually not overly effective in cleaning the anal orifice. They only succeeded in spreading the mess over a larger area of one's posterior thus resulting in an itchy asshole which invariably led to numerous skid marks on one's underwear. Only on special occasions, when the local parish priest or some other dignitary was coming for a visit, would one find the luxury of a roll of genuine store-bought toilet paper in most outhouses.

Outhouses were the butt (pardon the pun) of many crude jokes, particularly among elementary school children. They (the children, the jokes and the outhouses) were stinky, gross and dirty, a breeding place for flies, wasps, bees and sometimes rats and mice. But (pardon another pun) they were an endless source of amusement and pranks for some teenagers with tiny minds growing up in an age without television, internet, video games and iPods. For some reason the outhouse, being closely associated with Halloween, became the teenagers' instrument of choice for late night trickery on October 31.

One of the favorite no-brainer activities was sneaking around in the dark and tipping as many toilets as possible. I personally never participated in such juvenile behavior but heard endless boasting about it at school the next day. Besides, toilet tipping became so commonplace on Halloween that many adults took turns standing guard and scaring the crap out of teenagers who entered their back yards with evil intent. In any event toilet tipping was generally a harmless prank, and several of the same scoundrels who tipped the toilets the night of October 31 felt some remorse. Many took pity on the older residents of town and en masse came around the morning of November 1 to set the toilet back in its proper position. I even recall on one occasion a schoolmarm being so grateful that the "nice boys" set her outhouse upright that she paid each of them twenty-five cents for their thoughtful work. Thereafter, they joked about going into business year-round, tipping toilets at night then setting them upright the next day for a small fee.

The most adventuresome and innovative pranks relating to the toilet involved using one's rudimentary engineering skills to somehow load a toilet onto the back of an old Fargo half ton truck, haul it to some location where it would be winched onto a school, a gasoline service station, a home or left at the intersection of a couple of downtown streets. Another rather sneaky prank was, rather than tipping the toilet over, just moving the toilet three feet back, exposing the pit and giggling about how the inhabitants of the residence would fall in if they attempted to relieve their bowels or bladders in the darkness of night. Whoever developed that scheme is probably now working as the pin placement person at the local golf course. She always places the pin in the shittiest place on the green.

One of the more imaginative outhouse pranks, and one in which I must admit I was involved, occurred in late September 1955. One of the peculiarities of outhouses is that they are not connected to any sewer system. Depending on the frequency of use, the number of active users, the number of Eaton's catalogues and the depth of the original pit, the level of excrement would eventually reach near the top of the rough wooden toilet seat. In fact, on one occasion Cecilia and I attempted to use an outhouse in which the mound of turds and paper was actually above the level of the toilet seat, prompting us to wonder, "At what point does the owner say, '*I think it's high enough now.*'?"

In any event, depending on the variables previously mentioned, the outhouse hole would become full. Eventually, an owner had to either dig a new hole or hire someone to dig one for him, then have the toilet moved to the new location and fill the old hole with soil to reduce the odour which inevitably emanated from the human by-products deposited there.

Such was the problem for John McReady, a good natured, friendly elderly gentleman who lived with his wife in a small four room stucco house next to our hotel. Being retired many years, John had time on his hands, time to visit with and impress all the pre-teen and early teen boys with his wit, wisdom and stories during the summer school break and at the end of each school day when they were eager to find some excuse for avoiding their homework. John was seventy-four years old and in top physical and mental condition for his age. He decided to save some cash by digging the new toilet hole on his own over the space of a few weeks in September 1955.

This was an interesting project, particularly for our ragamuffin gang of ten to fifteen year olds. So each day after school we would gather around the toilet hole inspecting the progress as the hole got deeper and John's stories got more entertaining. After three days, when the hole was starting to reach the depth of three or four feet, at the end of the school day our group gathered round the hole noticing that John had piled up a few rocks beside the hole, and as we visited he gathered up one or two of the rocks, picking away at them with his finger nails and pointing out to us that there were tiny shiny flecks in the rocks, a possible sign of GOLD DUST, he said. Boys our age were easily impressed, but we weren't completely gullible either. We all genuinely enjoyed our encounters with John who was almost a grandfather figure to us. So, as a mark of respect for his age and in consideration of his friendship to us we all refrained from telling the old fellow that he was dreaming if he thought there was gold in those rocks.

We left it at that, went home for supper, then later that evening five of us gathered again to determine what kind of mischief we could conjure up. As we giggled and engaged in harmless horse-play common to young boys the topic of Mr. McReady's gold arose. My cousin Ernie remembered that his parents had some very authentic looking gold paint which shone quite vividly when it was applied to any object. Someone with a devious mind suggested that we get a selection of small stones, apply some gold paint to them and plant them in the partially dug toilet hole. Capital idea! It took very little time for us to find eight or ten golf ball to baseball sized rocks in a variety of shapes and to retrieve the small jar of specialty gold paint and a tiny paintbrush.

Ingenuity knows no bounds. In all of the larger rocks we painted veins of brilliant gold. Then someone suggested we find a few smaller pebbles, painting them completely to resemble solid gold nuggets. Within minutes we completed the art work, setting the rocks in a warm place for the paint to partially dry. We felt that it was not necessary for the paint to be completely tack-free, speculating that when we salted the mine the gold coloured rocks would look more genuine if some dirt clung to them.

By nine o'clock that evening it was dark enough for us to help Mr. McReady find some gold. Putting the "gold" ore in a small box and taking a flashlight to light the way, our giggling band made its way to John's back yard where we soon spotted the "mine shaft" covered by a thin sheet of plywood for the night. A few of us quickly and quietly removed the plywood while Ernie, being the ringleader, found the shovel and pick-axe ready for use the next day leaning against John's old garden tool shed. Within minutes Ernie had jumped down the hole, used the tools to dig a few assorted cavities at varying depths and randomly deposited pieces of our manufactured mother-lode. Then he carefully covered each of the new cavities with a little dirt, packing it down so the soil would not appear to be newly disturbed. The dirty deed was done. We quickly helped Ernie out of the hole, returned the tools to where we had found them, replaced the plywood over the hole and headed for home.

By then it was nearly ten o'clock in the evening and the next day was a school day, but we were so proud of our ingenious practical joke we shared the information with our parents who had a hearty laugh, but told us they suspected there would be little or no result from our efforts. Little did they know!

At school the following day we could barely contain ourselves, giggling and wondering about what treasures Mr. McReady might unearth. When the 3:30 school bell rang to end the school day I raced to the Post Office, where my dad was Postmaster, to find out the news. In all seriousness Dad related how early that afternoon Mr. McReady had come running to the post office showing off the rock samples excitedly describing how he had struck it rich. Fortunately, Dad being in on our little plot calmly suggested that the "ore" should be examined by an expert to verify its authenticity. It happened that the station agent, Cam Chernecki, was an amateur geologist as well as a terrific fiddler. Dad suggested that Mr. McReady visit Cam with his nugget samples to determine whether they were real gold.

We all know the result. Cam pulled out a pen knife, scrapped away a layer of paint and gave his assessment. According to Dad, Mr. McReady was sorely embarrassed by this turn of events so much so that I volunteered to go to visit him, turn myself in by telling him I was responsible for the prank, apologize for the situation and tell him we meant no harm. However, I followed Dad's advice which was to simply let the matter die as Mr. McReady would probably not relish revisiting the whole embarrassing situation and that in any event he likely had a very good idea who had played this rather elaborate practical joke on him.

So, Mr. McReady, wherever you are – sorry!

A Kuroki Education

*If there were no schools to take the
children away from home part of the
time, the insane asylums would be filled
with mothers. - Edgar W. Howe*

*Alicia, from my stories so far you might assume we youngsters
were always goofing off. But we spent only a very small part
of each day playing pranks on the senior citizens. For several
hours each day our job was to attend the Red Brick School
and to get an education.*

The British flag, the Union Jack, flew over that old
Red Brick School in Kuroki; every classroom had a
portrait of King George VI; then when he died in 1952
we had portraits of our pretty young Queen Elizabeth

II hanging on the wall. Every day in school we sang "God Save the King" (or Queen). We were taught that we were part of the British Empire, and we were proud when we looked at the globe or the Mercator map hanging near the blackboard on the classroom wall and saw the massive reach of the British Empire depicted in a deep pink. In the 1950's Canada was still a young country clinging to British traditions - in fact, by world standards even today it is a relatively young country.

Attending the old Red Brick School in Kuroki was quite different from going to school today. We walked four miles to school, uphill both ways, against the wind, forty below zero, winter and summer! I jest, but almost everyone walked to school. For me it was only four or five blocks, but some of my classmates walked a few miles each way. The trip to and from school each day was fairly routine, so I and my friends spiced it up with a variety of home grown entertainment. A game of kick the can – a beat-up Texaco or Havoline Oil can which we kicked all the way to school - was great fun at any time of the year, but spring was the most fun. Kuroki didn't have sewers and no real drainage system for spring run-off, so the ditches in town would be over-flowing and huge puddles of water, almost small lakes, some up to one hundred yards across would accumulate in parts of town. The largest of these was near the Saskatchewan Wheat Pool and Federal grain elevators, fortuitously close to my normal route to school. Often, after the spring melt, the heavy night frost left a thin sheet of smooth ice on the surface of these bodies of water. Being of scientific bent, on our way to school in the morning my friends and I often felt an obligation, if only for research purposes, to experiment, to test the ice on these ponds, just to be sure they would support the weight of an eight year old boy. The results of these experiments varied. Occasionally, the smooth ice would support us, but would crack ominously as we slid around trying to maintain our balance. More often, however, one or more of us would break through the thin ice and have to run home to mother with a boot or two full of icy cold water complaining that we were cold and needed a change of socks and shoes. Youthful scientific minds sometimes have to bear the burdens of cold, wet feet or endure the wrath of an angry mother.

From the autumn of 1949 when I started school until June of 1959 when I finished Grade 10 many things in Kuroki School stayed much the same – Third World same. There was no running water. Each morning the janitor would bring water from the municipal well and fill a huge crockery water jug which served as our water fountain. After every recess and lunch break the water fountain line-up was never ending. Since there was no running water there were no flush toilets. There were two wooden outhouses – one for males, one for females - some thirty yards to the right rear of the school. Where students washed their hands after using the toilet is beyond my recollection. It probably didn't happen. Some twenty or so yards from the outhouses there was a barn. Occasionally one or more students would ride a horse to school using the barn to accommodate the animal during the day. If fact, one of my friends named Michael and his older brother named Edward who lived over three miles from Kuroki often rode to school together on one horse in spring and fall. Then, during the winter they would often hitch the horse to a large home built toboggan to be pulled through the snowdrifts to and from school each day. At other times the brothers walked over three miles to and from school so, for them, there was some truth to having to walk four miles to and from school. Not that they did it uphill both ways and certainly not when it was forty degrees below zero.

During the ten years I attended Kuroki School every teacher taught several grades in their classroom. Having to prepare lessons for three or four grades each day was probably quite a strain on the teachers, but there were certain advantages for the students. For instance, while the teacher was instructing one of the other classes, you could work on your homework, read, or surreptitiously pass notes to one of your friends or one of the pretty girls on the other side of the classroom. When the teacher's back was turned or when he was concentrating on another grade you could float a paper airplane across the classroom, or you could exchange jokes with the person sitting behind or in front of you - until you were caught. You had to be judicious in your tom-foolery because if you were overly rambunctious you could be threatened with a few lashes of the strap or a generous whack with a yardstick across the palms of your hands, although that measure was not usually imposed except in the instances of lying, cheating, stealing or more serious crimes like murder or shooting spit-balls at the teacher. A few times I watched the strap being administered to certain offenders and was not keen to press my luck.

At times the teacher would ask the older students, the ones in the higher grades, to help the younger ones with their lessons. As well, when you were one of the younger ones you derived a certain pleasure in getting a preview of what was to come in future years. It wasn't so scary or difficult after all. Finally, one of the perks of having several grades in one classroom is that every day after lunch the teacher read a story to the younger students. Being in the same classroom, all the other grades participated in the listening. At times, at the urging of the students, especially when the story was reaching a climax or some special part, the teacher would continue reading until the afternoon recess break. At the time we all thought that we were getting away from doing classroom work, but upon looking back on it now perhaps the story time for all those years gave us a real appreciation for literature.

In the early days, the days without television, we sometimes listened to the radio in school. There were fewer sports teams and they were easier to follow, but we didn't see them. We listened to them on radio. One of the highlights of the year was when the World Series of baseball was being played. Many of the games were played during school hours and it became a special treat when we were able to convince the teacher that we should take time from our hard work for the whole class to listen to the game. It seemed that in the 1950's almost every year The New York Yankees and the Brooklyn Dodgers met in the finals. I remember when I first listened to some of the World Series games with my Father. He always cheered for the Brooklyn Dodgers. When I asked him why, he told me that the New York Yankees had a strong win record and that he had a habit of cheering for the underdog – the Dodgers. To start with I followed his lead, cheering wildly for the Dodgers. A few years later I switched to the Pittsburgh Pirates; then when Canada got its own teams my allegiance went to the Toronto Blue Jays.

Besides the enjoyment of listening to World Series games on the school radio we also listened to occasional educational programming on the CBC network. The most common was the school music programming led by *Rj Staples, Music Director for the Saskatchewan Department of Education. In many small schools there was no teacher who had musical training or who could play any instrument, so the provincially broadcast music program was an effort to give the "unwashed" a tiny bit of culture. However, in Kuroki School, Mrs. Simmonds, who was quite proficient on the piano, provided us with some choral instruction. We even had rudimentary music lessons with everyone trying their hand at the tonnette, a type of inexpensive wooden or plastic flute. When expertly played, the tonnette has quite a beautiful sound, but few of us learned to play it well. I recall much squawking and screeching when Mrs. Simmonds formed a tonnette band to perform at one Christmas concert. In fact, the web site "On Music Dictionary" states that *the Tonnette has a very pleasant sound, not unlike a recorder or flute. Overblowing is possible to extend the range, but that sound is not entirely pleasing when performed by a novice and somewhat difficult to control.* "Not entirely pleasing" is the understatement of the twentieth century. The sound alluded to may be likened to the sound a goose would make when laying an oversized egg!

In addition to the small, rudimentary music program, at the beginning of each day we sang *O Canada* and at the end of each day we sang *God Save the Queen*, but we also recited the Lord's Prayer at the beginning of each school day. Additionally, not yet being politically correct, just before Christmas we had something called a "Christmas Concert" where we sang songs and had pageants about Christ's birth, the

Three Wise Men and Peace on Earth. What were they thinking? Were they trying to turn us into Christians? One quotation by an unknown author seems appropriate here: "As long as there are tests in schools, there will be prayer in schools."

*I recall once asking a teacher what the initials Rj stood for in the name "Rj Staples". Apparently Rj's parents were expecting a girl. They had picked out girl's names with the initials R. and J. When a boy was born they decided to name him Rj; that is why the R is upper case and the J is lower case. So the Rj is not his initials; it is his name. Anyway, that's what the teacher said!

My Life as a Gunslinger

The fascination of shooting as a sport depends almost wholly on whether you are at the right or wrong end of the gun
- P. G. Wodehouse, The Adventures of Sally

One comedian, when describing the difference between Canadians and Americans, said that a Canadian is an unarmed American with health care. Americans are enamoured with their firearms and they pay dearly for it with firearm related deaths in the U.S.A. averaging approximately eighty-seven people each day or about thirty-two thousand per year. Canadians once regarded firearms as commonplace, utilitarian objects, particularly in rural areas to protect their cattle, sheep and chickens from predators such as foxes and coyotes as well as a means to control the gopher population. Furthermore, up until the middle of the twentieth century duck, goose, deer, moose and elk hunting often provided – and still do provide – rural residents and First Nations citizens with a valuable source of protein. However, the advent of urbanization, larger agri-business farms, a sparse rural population and gun control has resulted in fewer Canadians regarding guns as necessary for everyday life in modern society.

In Kuroki, when I was growing up, every boy and even a few girls had toy pistols, rifles, and six-guns, and played "war" and "Cowboys and Indians", but present day Canadian parents are less permissive of children handling toy firearms. It has been many years since I have seen children playing with toy guns. Instead, parents allow them to imagine wreaking havoc with firearms via video games and watching violent movies.

My own first experience with a real firearm was quite accidental. Boys, and probably girls, aged five, six or seven are quite curious. They snoop around in every nook and cranny to find new, delightful and some-times dangerous objects. I was no exception. Kuroki Hotel was not huge, but to a six year old it seemed gigantic with numerous stairwells, closets, secret pas-sages and rooms to explore. Upstairs, there were eleven rooms plus a bathroom. One of the rooms we called the "Spare Room". It was never rented out or used as a bedroom. Instead, it became a storage room, a place where we took our baths in a large galvanized metal tub before the days of running water, and a place where curious children loved to snoop, to see what treasures could be hidden there.

It was 1950; I was six years old; we had only lived in Kuroki Hotel for a short time. To a six year old the hotel was a massive structure with many treasures, caches of memorabilia and junk to be discovered. The spare room might house some of these hidden delights. I had to find out. One day around noon while Mom and Granny were busily preparing and serving the noon meal to several hotel guests, I and my five year old brother Don took advantage of the opportunity to do a little exploring. The spare room was a logical place to start. In the spare room there were a few shelves, many corrugated cardboard boxes and a few old wooden storage units with doors on them. We climbed over a few boxes and made our way to one corner of the room where stood a smaller flimsy white storage unit with an unlocked door. It didn't take long. Opening the door and moving a few uninteresting pieces of junk to the side, to our delight we saw what appeared to be a genuine six-gun. Immediately, before Don could claim it as his, I picked it up saying that I had found it. Appearing quite authentic, it was a dark, blue-grey gunmetal colour, feeling quite heavy for my six year old hands. You can imagine my excitement at discovering such a treasure. I certainly did not realize the gravity of the situation, the potential danger of the object I was handling, or even whether it was loaded. I immediately wanted to share the information about my newfound treasure with Mom and Granny. So, running down the back staircase as fast as my little legs would carry me, I rushed through the kitchen and into the hotel dining room where Mom and Granny were waiting on guests. I waved the firearm in front of them excitedly telling everyone of the great discovery I had unearthed. My mother was horrified and embarrassed, quickly taking the gun from my hands, ushering me into the kitchen and telling me never to touch that gun again. Who knows what the guests thought of the scene?

Handguns were and continue to be illegal for the average citizen in Canada unless certain very stringent conditions are met. I'm not sure if my dad had a permit or what his reasons were for possessing the gun. Perhaps he had picked it up when he was in the army; maybe he bought it for some target shooting when he was on the farm; or perhaps he thought that being a hotel owner-businessman would make him and his family the target of thieves, so he decided to keep some deterrent around. I never knew, and I was too young to understand. In any event, I knew that I was never to touch that gun again, that it was real, and that it could kill someone. I also knew that my mother sternly informed my dad to secure the firearm and to quickly dispose of it. It wasn't until many years later, when I was in my teens, that I learned from Dad that he had discussed the issue with an RCMP officer who purchased it from him.

Fortunately my initial gun slinging experience did not result in injury or death. Nor did it deter me from dreams of riding the range with Roy Rogers, Gene Autry or The Lone Ranger with six-guns at my side. Until the age of ten or so, I and my playmates played with toy guns and rifles as often as we played in the sand pile with toy trucks, cars and farm machinery. But before I entered my teens I had dreams of owning my first BB gun. Almost every western comic book – in addition to the mandatory "Charles Atlas" bodybuilding ad - contained at least one page with an advertisement for a Daisy Air Rifle, a BB gun. I doubted I would ever be a strongman, but I was sure I could be a cowboy if only I had a Daisy Air Rifle. The comic book ads told me so, and by the age of eleven Don and I had managed to convince, nag or badger our dad of our maturity and our readiness to be owners of a BB gun. And once we got our Air Rifle we never shot out anyone's eyes, although a couple sparrows and gophers met their demise at our hands. When I think about it now, why would anyone want to shoot a sparrow? After a year or so the gun lost much of its power, so we used it mainly for target practice. Then, after the BB gun became quite harmless I remember shooting Don in the butt on one occasion, and early one Saturday morning a cow grazing on CNR property near town felt a BB on its hind quarters. Neither my brother Don nor the bovine have ever forgiven me for my thoughtless actions.

Very soon the BB rifle became boring, and by the age of twelve, every day and every night I dreamt of owning a real .22 calibre rifle. It took a pile of whining to convince Dad I was old and mature enough to be the owner of a .22 calibre rifle – "all the other boys have one." Finally, in the summer of 1957, Dad relented. Don and I became the proud owners of a repeating bolt action .22 calibre rifle purchased through Simpsons-Sears mail order catalogue (prior to its becoming toilet paper).

We were not allowed to use that rifle without Dad's supervision that first summer. He wanted to be sure we were aware of its lethal power and that we took appropriate safety precautions. That message became much louder and much clearer when we heard of an accidental shooting death in Wadena. A fourteen year old boy was accidentally shot in the head by a friend and hunting companion as four of them walked through the bush stalking rabbits. There were other firearms accidents, and deaths, which Dad and Mom always brought to our attention to make us aware of our responsibilities when we went out with our .22 rifle.

In later years, after I was married, I purchased a single shot .22 Remington rifle for target shooting. Then in 1967 I bought a shotgun for duck and upland game hunting. I used that for four years, even scaring a few ducks and prairie chickens. Finally I purchased a modified Lee Enfield 303 rifle for deer hunting – I never went deer hunting and never used that rifle except once or twice on targets. For years those three guns sat idle in our rumpus room. Eventually, in the 1970's and 1980's stricter gun control legislation was passed in Canada leading me to consider disposing of my arsenal. Living in the city of Regina where the guns never were used, at the risk of offending the National Rifle Association and Charlton Heston, in 1987 I sold my cache of weaponry to a local gun club before it could be pried from my cold dead hands.

I have always wondered why men are enthralled with guns so much more than women until one day when I was searching for appropriate quotes and proverbs for my stories I came across a quotation from Lorrie Moore's, *Like Life* which provides a logical explanation: "*Guns, she was reminded then, were not for girls. They were for boys. They were invented by boys. They were invented by boys who had never gotten over their disappointment that accompanying their own orgasm there wasn't a big boom sound.*"

Learning to Smoke

To cease smoking is the easiest thing I ever did. I ought to know because I've done it a thousand times. - Mark Twain

Sometimes we weren't out plinking with our BB guns or .22 rifles. And sometimes we weren't playing pranks on older folks. We engaged in some other questionable practices. Sad to say, Alicia, smoking was one of them. Today's school system and media educate youth on the harmful effects of cigarette smoke, but when I was growing up it was a different story.

In the 1950's smoking was mandatory. Everyone did it, and you did too even if you never lit up. Second-hand smoke was at kitchen tables, in bedrooms, in cars, buses and airplanes (Who thought that was a good idea?), in dance halls, beer parlours, restaurants, schools – everywhere. By the time you were five years old you were addicted to nicotine simply by virtue of being alive. Not only were you hooked; you wanted to be hooked. It was cool, sophisticated and even healthy. Full page magazine ads displayed tough, swarthy cowboys on spirited horses breathing fresh mountain air and taking a break to enjoy the fresh clean taste of Marlboro cigarettes. One ad went so far as to say: More doctors smoke Camels than any other cigarette. And one Lucky Strike ad told us that 20,679 physicians say, "Luckies are less irritating." Not to be outdone, a Viceroy Cigarette ad showed a dentist saying, "As your dentist, I would recommend Viceroys." I guess they make your teeth look whiter and your breath smell fresher!

When we got our first black and white 21 inch console Zenith television in 1958 we could watch reporters, entertainers and game show hosts puff away while they worked; then during a commercial break we could watch the same game show hosts promote the smooth "well-mannered" taste of Du Maurier cigarettes. In movies and television shows all the popular actors and actresses of the day lit up as they played their roles. It was an expected glamorous part of the show. How an unsavory habit like cigarette smoking came to be associated with elegance, sophistication, and glamour is a testament to the ingenuity of the marketing and advertising industry as well as the conscience and scruples-barren tobacco industry. To this day, the marketing of e-cigarettes and various candy flavoured tobaccos is targeting the most impressionable and vulnerable in our society, our youth, to ensure they become hooked on nicotine thus ensuring a never-ending income stream for the tobacco barons.

My own first smoking attempt was at Uncle Walter's house in about 1950. My parents, my brother Don and I were visiting Uncle Walter and his family in their small three room house in Kuroki. The adults sat in the family room which doubled as the kids' bedroom, men smoking and women visiting. The older children played outside while we young kids played in the parents' bedroom. My cousin Lornie and I were six years old and we knew all about how to smoke. We had watched our fathers do it since we were in diapers so we knew exactly what to do. We weren't about to ask our dads for a cigarette, so we found some newspaper, tore it in strips about the length of a cigarette and rolled it loosely to look like a cigarette. It wasn't difficult to procure matches. They were everywhere for the convenience of smokers. Quietly sneaking into the bedroom closet we managed to light a match and hold it to the newspaper cigarette which I held in my mouth ready to inhale that first intoxicating puff of smoke. Not all went according to plan. The dry newspaper, being highly combustible, burst into flames; and as I inhaled my first deep breath of the anticipated sweet cigarette smoke the loosely rolled newspaper funneled red-hot ashes and flames into my mouth. Simultaneously dropping the "cigarette", coughing and crying I ran from the room into my mother's arms. Luckily we didn't burn the house down, but I do recall a burning sensation on my posterior resulting from my father's disgust at my behavior on that day.

In the mid-1950's a few radical scientists, researchers and doctors began to link smoking to lung cancer and respiratory diseases, but their fear-mongering was largely discounted as something which *might* happen in the future whereas today we had to build bomb shelters and learn how to hide under school desks, away from windows while preparing for imminent nuclear annihilation by the Soviet regime. Fear of being blasted into Kingdom Come made people so jumpy they needed a cigarette to calm their nerves.

We had great smoking role models too. At recess time our teacher, John Tymko would stoke the old coal furnace in the school basement while sucking on his pipe. We grade six and seven boys stood around watching him while he impressed us with wild stories about his boyhood. Then, after school we could watch the town gentlemen with their tobacco tar-stained fingers and nicotine-brown moustaches visit on street corners while hand-rolling cigarettes using Chanticleer Cigarette Papers and Ogden Fine Cut Tobacco.

My own repeat foray into the world of smoking came in 1955 at the age of eleven. My younger brother, Don, and his older friend, Gary, had been sneaking the odd cigarette for a couple of weeks, and they wanted to share their new-found sinful pleasure with me. They invited me into an abandoned old horse-drawn trailer previously used by a travelling Watkins dealer for hauling, distributing and selling home care products, liniments and spices. They had stashed a few cigarettes there under the loose board of a wooden seat. It was the perfect place for ten to thirteen year olds to sneak a quick smoke. That worked for a week or two until our mother smelled cigarette smoke on Don and me, ratted on us to Dad resulting in a good lecture about the evils of smoking and the practise of a little reverse psychology.

First Dad told us that if we wanted to smoke we had better do it at home, so we wouldn't burn down someone's home. In fact he said he would supply the cigarettes and then went on to pull out a couple of big cigars, giving us one each and encouraging us to enjoy them with him and inhale deeply. Joylessly, I sucked on that big stogie for five or ten minutes while Dad and Uncle "taught" us how to savor the real flavor of a good smoke. What fun is there in smoking if you have to do it without skulking around back alleys and old abandoned buildings evading the watchful eyes of adults? The reverse psychology appeared to have achieved its intended purpose on me, at least for a few years. I quit the filthy habit until Grade eleven.

Then in 1958 I attended Grade eleven at St. Joseph's College, Christian Brother's boarding school in Yorkton, Saskatchewan where smoking was common among the students. We were permitted to smoke in the school yard, but Saskatchewan winters can be rather harsh so, in their wisdom, rather than trying to prevent the students from smoking, the Christian Brothers provided a smoking room which we used daily for card playing and smoking. I guess in the 1950's it was the Christian thing to do. At old St. Joe's cigarettes were a valuable type of currency. Meal time would net you from one to three Export A's if you were willing to give up your dessert.

Through high school, summer jobs and my four years at the University of Saskatchewan I continued my evil ways, sucking up the smoke from about three packs of Craven "A's" each week. When I married Cecilia in 1964 she regularly reminded me about my filthy, stinky routine and prevailed upon me to quit. In fact, for two or three months at a time I was able to kick the habit, but each time I returned convincing myself that a few cigarettes wouldn't hurt me. Teaching at Hanley Composite High School in Hanley, Saskatchewan for five years from 1965 to 1970 did nothing to help me quit my addictive habit. Although the students in Hanley were not permitted to smoke, if any of them dared knock on the staff room door at recess or lunch hour they were greeted by a thick cloud of blue smoke. Do not do as I do; do as I say!

Over the next few years from 1970 until 1976 I was employed as a Manpower Counselor with the Department of Manpower and Immigration in Prince Albert, Saskatchewan. All job and career counselors had ashtrays at their desks, smoked with their clientele and were rude enough to puff away when job-counseling non-smokers. I am guilty. I tried to change my ways by giving up the filthy habit for a few weeks at a time, always using a substitute such as chewing gum or gnawing on a toothpick to keep my mind off the cigarettes. During one such attempt at quitting smoking I chewed on a toothpick for almost every waking hour of the day. My toothpick addiction became almost as disagreeable as my previous smoking habit prompting one of my co-workers to tease that I might not die of lung cancer, but I could develop a serious case of Dutch elm disease.

Finally in about 1973 Manpower and Immigration encouraged non-smoking campaigns and prohibited Manpower employees from smoking in front of clientele. At about the same time an intensive anti-smoking and health education campaign was introduced into the public school system. One day our son, Greg came home in tears asking his Mom if his Dad was going to die of cancer because he was a smoker. That experience gave me some pause about my own smoking habit.

Greg's fear of my imminent demise as well as the Federal Government's putting a damper on workplace smoking gave me impetus to give up my fondness for tobacco. Then in late 1973 a friend and co-worker came to me with a novel proposal: that we form a mutual non-smoking pact. The conditions of that pact were that the first one of us to take up smoking again would have to pay the exorbitant sum of five dollars cash to the non-smoker. In return, the non-smoker would provide the smoker with a tersely worded letter telling him what a weak-willed, good-for-nothing snake-in-the-grass bastard he was for revisiting the abhorrent, addictive habit. That pact was formed forty-two years ago, and I have never taken up the habit and to my knowledge neither has he. I toast him for proposing this ingenious incentive for both of us. However, forty-two years is a long time for an old mind to remember details of the agreement. As I wrote these words I recalled that over the past forty-two years I had occasionally shared a cigarette with a friend or relative while enjoying a cocktail. Very naughty, even though I resolved never to take up the filthy habit, and I never will. However, by having those few cigarettes I have likely broken our agreement and owe him five dollars, so just before Christmas 2014 I sent him a Christmas card with a letter explaining my guilt and enclosing a crisp new five dollar bill.

I await his nasty letter to me – I hope he doesn't expect me to pay interest for forty-two years.

Note: The best way to stop smoking is to carry wet matches.

Healthcare – "Schmelthcare"

The doctor of the future will give no medicine but will interest his patients in the care of the human frame, in diet and in the cause and prevention of disease. - Thomas Edison

The topic of smoking and its effects on our health invariably leads to some interesting debates about health care. In Canada we often take our health care system for granted, thinking we can abuse our bodies then expect the doctors and the "system" to take care of us. We need to care for our Medicare system as much as we need to care for ourselves. We didn't always have a universal health care system in Canada. It was not until December 1966 that the Parliament of Canada passed the federal Medicare legislation that implemented full Medicare across Canada. That Act became effective in 1968 and was fully implemented in all provinces by 1972. Before that, in the 1950's we were often our own doctors and nurses – we ministered to ourselves.

The Americans say they've got the best health care system in the world, and it probably is, for those who are able to afford it. In Canada our universal health care system is one of the best in the world, but it needs tweaking and updating too. Doesn't matter what health care system we have, eventually we die. Doctors and nurses get sick and die too. In my opinion not enough attention or resources are devoted to promoting and advocating lifestyle changes needed to keep us healthy. Instead, it seems that much of our health care system, rather than being used to keep people healthy, is devoted to keeping people alive – people who in many cases are ready to die, want to die and who would have died except for some heroic medical intervention which keeps them alive to suffer almost endlessly. To me that's not health "care". Sounds more like legalized torture.

Long before our modern health care system and before people had access to doctors and hospitals, many people with illnesses which can now be remedied easily with antibiotics or simple surgery succumbed to their maladies and passed away. This accounts for the fact that I never knew either of my grandfathers; they both died at an early age of rather routine ailments leaving my grandmothers as widows to raise large families on their own.

The general public, particularly those living on farms or more remote small towns in the early part of the twentieth century, did not have easy access to health care or medicines, so they fended for themselves using home remedies handed down from generation to generation by word of mouth or simply by trial and error. Even as late as the 1950's the primary products in most home medicine cabinets were Watkins products, aspirin, tincture of iodine, and some band-aids. For coughs and colds there were Smith Brothers Wild Cherry or Black Licorice cough drops and Vicks VapoRub, whereas for severe bronchial congestion one common home remedy was the mustard plaster which occasionally caused severe skin burns when left on the chest for too long. In case of a cut, bruise, burn or insect bite Watkins Petro-Carbo Salve was always close at hand. For boils, various skin infections and rashes a homemade poultice could work wonders.

Measles and mumps were still common childhood diseases, and it was not until 1955 that the Salk polio vaccine was approved for public immunization. If something really terrible happened people tried to find a doctor, but for what they considered minor injuries they did whatever they could to patch themselves up or cure themselves of their disease. In these pages I could occasionally be accused of hyperbole, but without stretching the truth I can say that in his lifetime my father used a forty-five gallon drum or more of rubbing alcohol as treatment for everything from chronic dandruff to aching muscles to disinfecting wounds. He even used it as a haemorrhoidal treatment even though when he applied it he yowled from the burning pain. When he told my sister, Barbara, about this she became very bossy and insisted he cease the rubbing alcohol treatment and try Preparation H or some similar product. In summary, if it hurt, itched or bled Dad poured rubbing alcohol on it and proclaimed its curative powers to anyone who would listen. Then for his internal wounds he used alcohol with a slightly different formula – it was called moonshine.

Another common curative for anything that ails you, according to Granny and Aunt Elsie, was something they called "kefir", a kind of homemade yoghurt which they produced at home on the window sill. For years they made it, drank it daily and tried to promote it as an elixir. Amazingly, they survived! Years later I read about the dangers of making and consuming the stuff. Apparently some pretty ugly bacteria are produced if you do it wrong.

Having my raging case of acne I personally experienced one of Granny's home remedies. It was a mixture of charcoal, sulfur and honey which I was to apply to my face leaving it there for several hours each day. It may have worked, but who knows? I applied the sticky mess on a couple of occasions, but dared not leave the house because of the sight and smell of the stuff. A black goop, having a faint rotten egg smell, it was something one would not classify as Cover Girl make-up. I gave up on it long before I could really experience its curative effects.

So, the rubbing alcohol, kefir and acne treatments were do-it-yourself projects, but occasionally there were more serious issues which needed medical attention. Some such medical maladies were the sprains, muscle tears, muscle spasms, neck and back problems together with any related joint and muscle complaints. Residents of rural areas and smaller towns had little or no access to qualified chiropractors, massage therapists or physiotherapists, but they were not without some terrific inexpensive therapy. One such miracle worker was Ivor Ilves of the Margo district in Saskatchewan. I never experienced his curative healing touch, but both my parents and some of my brothers and sisters have given thanks for his therapeutic hands.

One such occasion was in the spring of 1957. My brother Jim, being nearly one year old, had just begun to learn to walk, but without warning one morning he suddenly refused to lower his left leg either because he suffered some unknown injury to it or because of some unknown congenital defect. After a few days of no change to his behavior and with Jim still refusing to lower his left leg, not unlike a male dog wanting to urinate, my parents became worried about him. Ivor Ilves to the rescue!

Dad phoned Ivor, who had a small farm just twelve or so miles from Kuroki Hotel, making an appointment for him to see little Jimmy. When they arrived they were not alone. The humble farm house was filled with all sorts of limping and aching people waiting for treatment, but before long it was Jim's turn. Ivor looked at him, questioned my parents about his condition and quickly went to work feeling, manipulating and gently massaging little Jim's hip joint and muscles. Within an hour Jim's leg seemed to be working properly again. When he was asked to stand he did so. After Mrs. Ilves treated them to some coffee and some sweets Dad paid Mr. Ilves the exorbitant sum of one dollar and they were on their way home. In the 1950's Ivor Ilves' standard charge was one dollar per treatment unless it involved a prolonged or highly complex procedure when he might double the price.

At home for the next day Jim seemed to do fine, slightly favoring that left leg, but using it quite normally until the following morning when there was an instant replay of Jim's refusal to stand on his left leg despite my parents' pleadings. With that turn of events Dad decided to see if Ivor would consent to coming to live for five days in one of our vacant rooms in Kuroki Hotel giving Jim his healing therapy on a more intensive schedule. Whatever miracles Mr. Ilves performed that week have endured to this day. My brother Jim continues to be steady on both legs even at his ripe old age of fifty-eight, except for the times when he samples excessive amounts of fine Scotch whiskey. I never did discover what Dad paid for Ivor Ilves' five days of live-in therapy, but whatever it was Jim says for him it was worth every penny.

Not all people suffered from physical aches and pains. Some suffered from hypochondria or psychological and emotional trauma.

Enter the witch doctor, seer, shaman or mystic! Yep, we had those in the 1950's. They did everything: ear candling, removing spells, developing potions, curing depression, eradicating phobias, stopping bed wetting and engaging in match-making for the lovelorn. Both my brother Don and I had encounters with one of these women. I don't remember what age I was, probably about five or six, but I recall that for some reason I had an inordinate fear of water. I feared going into a boat or venturing near larger bodies of water. I even feared Dad's driving through large puddles of water on the road after heavy rains. I used to scream so hysterically when I encountered these "water hazards" that my parents decided to take me to a see a renowned mystic in the Quill Lake district of Saskatchewan. I was too young to remember all of her incantations, prayers and ministrations but I remember candles, the smell of incense, prayers and consultations with Mom and Dad. When we left she gave my parents a large green bottle of some kind of potion for me to consume an ounce or so daily. It looked like some clear liquid with either small pieces of wax and/or lemon floating in it and it had a somewhat waxy taste and feel – not unpleasant as I recall. In any event, I do not remember how much of the potion I drank or how long it took for its powers to rid me of my phobia, but I was cured. To this day I enjoy boating, swimming, fishing, snorkeling and just being around water. The only water hazards I continue to fear are those on the golf course.

Witch doctors, home remedies and the practice of alternative medicines prevail to the present day. There continue to be situations where people suffer from certain diseases which modern health care still cannot properly or completely cure. When people are desperate they will search for solutions and cures anywhere. Evidence the current trend toward medical marijuana, both home-grown and physician prescribed. Rather than depend on pain killers for their arthritis, rheumatism and war wounds the population will turn to bee stings as a cure for arthritis, ginger as an anti-inflammatory and good old fashioned whiskey for their war wounds.

Modern medicine is great, improving and pro-longing countless lives, but home remedies and traditional medicines are often worth trying. I toast your good health!

Flight of Fancy

Once you have tasted flight, you will forever walk the earth with your eyes turned skyward, for there you have been, and there you will always long to return. - Leonardo da Vinci

Speaking of health care reminds me that one of my Mother's brothers, Dr Nicholas Mazer, was a dentist. Uncle Nick was born December 13, 1922 and was still a teenager when the Second World War started. Then, in June of 1942 at the age of nineteen, with the war still raging, he enlisted in the Royal Canadian Air Force. He was sent overseas to serve as a bomb aimer on a Lancaster Bomber flying from London to various strategic targets in Germany to help defeat Hitler and the Nazis.

Left to right: Warrant Officer/Wireless Operator,
Krivka; Bomb Aimer, Nick Mazer (my Uncle);
Flight Officer/Navigator, Roy Taylor; Flight Officer/
Pilot, George Pauli; Sergeant/Rear Gunner, "Scottie"
Scott; Sergeant/Mid-Upper Gunner, Del Harper;
Sergeant/Flight Engineer, Harry Willmore (RAF)

After serving honourably in the war he studied dentistry at McGill University in Montreal. During his
summer breaks Uncle Nick often spent time with us at
Kuroki hotel. Then, after graduating from the dental
college in 1954 he made Kuroki hotel his home base
and began part-time dental practices in Kelvington and
Foam Lake some twenty-three miles north and south

of Kuroki. On weekends and holidays he would often do extractions and fillings in one of the spare rooms in our hotel using a small portable dentist's drill which he left in Kuroki and a black bag full of dental instruments which he carried with him. He provided these dental services at no charge for his relatives and for a small fee for other residents of the Kuroki area.

In 1956 Uncle Nick married a pretty lady named Helen. Their marriage took place in St. Helen's Roman Catholic Church in Kuroki where I, my brother Don, and my cousins Ernie and Lornie were altar servers for their wedding. After the ceremony a reception took place right in our Kuroki hotel. So, I had a war hero dentist uncle who brought home a new Aunt. Life was exciting, but for me it was going to get better. My Uncle Nick became an airplane pilot!

Orville and Wilbur Wright had no idea what they started when in 1903 they caused a heavier-than-air machine to rise from the earth, fly a short distance and land without crashing. Just ten years later, in January 1914 the first ever scheduled flight with a paying passenger took place. The airline industry has grown exponentially since then. In 2013, according to Ask.com, there were between 8,000 and 13,000 planes in the air at all times with approximately 93,000 daily flights originating from about 9,000 airports around the globe.

Allegedly, in the early 1950's planes occasionally even flew over and around our tiny hamlet of Kuroki. I say "allegedly" because when we were outdoors playing hockey in winter or baseball in summer, my playmates talked about seeing planes flying overhead. They would point at them and show me where they were in the sky, but it was to no avail. Generally, I saw nothing where they pointed. There is an Italian proverb: seeing is believing. I had no trouble believing in airplanes. I knew they existed. I saw them in pictures. I just never saw them in the air until one clear, cold day in March 1953 while we played hockey. That day a very low flying shiny silvery plane circled over town. I actually saw it. What a great day!

Then in the autumn of 1954 things took a turn for me. One day my Fifth Grade teacher, John Tymko noticed that I was straining to see the blackboard. He asked me to stand by my desk; putting his hand on my shoulder, he asked me to read what was written on the blackboard. I couldn't do it. You can't read what you can't see. He told me that I probably needed prescription eyeglasses and to tell my parents to get my vision tested. Routine vision testing of children did not occur in the early 1950's. Airplanes and chalk scribbling on blackboards were not the only things I couldn't see. I had no idea that with my uncorrected vision I was nearly legally blind, at least severely myopic. How was I to know that most other folks had 20/20 vision and that mine was about 20/200 in one eye and 20/400 in the other? Shortly thereafter I got my first pair of thick lens eyeglasses enabling me to see the blackboard in school as well as to see airplanes, birds, butterflies and all sorts of God's beautiful creatures. Life was amazing, but it would get better! I would not only see airplanes; I would fly in one.

When I was growing up, Sundays were "church" days and family days. After Mass we would often pack a picnic lunch, go for a ride in the country to explore, hike, play games, pick berries and mushrooms or just loll around on a blanket. Other times we would plan a special trip to visit one of my amazing Uncles and Aunts. One Sunday in June, 1961 our family, which by now had grown to eight of us - Dad, Mom, me, Don, Barbara, Margaret, Jim and little John, who was born in 1959 – all piled into our 1957 copper coloured Chevrolet Bel Air and travelled to Kamsack to visit Uncle Nick and Aunt Helen.

After Uncle Nick married my new Auntie Helen they had moved to Kamsack, Saskatchewan where Uncle Nick started his first real "permanent" dentistry practice from 1957 to 1965. There, because of his war experiences and his love of flying, Uncle Nick became actively involved in aviation. For several years he was Commander of the Kamsack Air Cadets. As well, he and several other men from Kamsack took flying lessons and obtained their pilot's licences. He also joined a flying club and, in 1960, together with twelve other flying enthusiasts, bought a small single engine plane.

I remember very little of what transpired at Uncle Nick's home that day – the war stories, the visiting, the joking, the eating, the partying and the games. Those things always happened whenever we visited with any one of my amazing uncles. But when Uncle Nick casually said, "Do you want to see my plane and go for a ride?" on that beautiful cloudless day in 1961 I was in for a memorable thrill ride.

When Dad, Don, Uncle Nick and I arrived at the Kamsack air field, Uncle led us directly into the open front hangar to the little craft which we were soon to board for the trip of a lifetime. It was a cream coloured aircraft with red trim. To my amazement, rather than being constructed of wood or metal, this flying machine had a wood and metal frame covered in a fabric which looked like a thin, but sturdy canvass material. Uncle told us that many light aircraft constructed prior to 1950 were fabric covered and wood framed, keeping them as light as possible. He went on to explain that in early aircraft saving weight was very important. As well, in order to save weight, most small planes in those days didn't have electric starters or heavy lead batteries. He said that he would start the engine by manually hand-cranking the propeller. Next, before starting the plane, Uncle took each of us into the plane separately. It was a two-seater with the passenger riding behind the pilot. As this was our first flying experience he knew that we were nervous so he took his time to explain each of the gadgets and instruments as well as their purpose. Since Dad had flown before, he gave the flight opportunity to his two eldest sons. Today was going to be a special day for Don and me. We would both have an opportunity to experience what a bird feels, the miracle of flight.

Before I knew it we were taxiing down the grassy runway and taking off. The exhilaration of the acceleration, the liftoff, the feeling of utter lightness and freedom are indescribable. The tiny craft, not pressurized or insulated in any way, produced a deafening roar upon acceleration and takeoff. Within seconds, for the first time in my life I saw people, automobiles, houses and farms below me getting smaller and smaller. Slowly we circled over the town. Soon there were tiny toy trains, cars, houses and people far below us. Uncle busied himself by pulling on the joystick, cranking levers, turning knobs and reading instruments. In a few minutes, reaching cruising altitude, Uncle eased back on the throttle and the plane became somewhat quieter, but to communicate we still had to shout at one another. He pointed out various landmarks, buildings, farms and interesting landscapes. Then came the part I will never forget. Uncle told me he was going to show me how he could land the plane if the engine failed. Advising me that he would almost turn the engine off, just keeping it running at a slow idle, he told me to pick out a landing spot that looked relatively flat (maybe a farmer's field) and away from trees and power and telephone lines. He re-emphasized that power and phone lines were very dangerous for planes performing unscheduled takeoffs and landings. Uncle eased back on the throttle even more. The plane quieted and we were in heaven, floating and soaring like butterflies or angels. I picked out an open farmer's field and pointed it out to Uncle Nick. He smiled and nodded at me. On this calm, clear day the light aircraft slowly and quietly drifted toward the earth. I was in awe as we made a wide circle, gently gliding toward the field I had pointed out until we came within thirty feet of the ground; then Uncle opened the throttle and pulled back on the joy stick. The engine roared into action, and we again climbed into the sky.

Since that day some fifty-five years ago I have relived that first flight many times over in my daydreams and my night dreams. But I am always wary of power lines. They stuck in my mind. Ever since that first flight, countless times in the middle of the night I have stretched out my arms, and slowly, gently, miraculously I have risen into the air, like Peter Pan, soaring over rooftops, trees, lakes, mountains and meadows. I have even soared into outer space and seen unfathomably beautiful moons, galaxies, stars and nebulae – there are no power lines in outer space. At other times I am indoors; in my dreams I stretch out my arms and slowly rise and soar around the room, always avoiding the chandelier. Often the dreams are in Technicolor, so real that when I awake I sometimes wonder if life is a dream, and the dream was reality.

Uncle Nick died of a heart attack at the young age of 63 on July 17, 1986. He is now soaring in the heavens; some day we will join him. Until then I shall be forever grateful for his kindness in introducing me to the miracle of flight.

Saturday Night Rassling

Most people gaze neither into the past nor the future: they explore neither truth nor lies. They gaze at the television. - Radiohead

Back in the early 1950's the Second World War was still fresh in people's minds. *(Remember, Alicia, I was born during that war.)* We were grateful to my Uncle who returned from the war and to many others who died to protect our freedom. But time tends to make people forget the debt that we owe the brave soldiers, airmen and seamen who helped to defeat the Nazis. Now we immerse ourselves in technology, tending to forget the stories of the past and the heroes who saved our freedom. We now take technology for granted, but in the early 1950's, particularly in Saskatchewan, it was just being introduced. One of those pieces of technology entertains us and sometimes makes us mindless. That marvelous technological breakthrough was the miracle of television which we continue to adore.

Television was one of the coolest, terrific-est, super-greatest best inventions of the 20th century. It was really the start of our romance with technology, the beginnings of our connectedness with machines and the end of our connectedness with people. Prior to television people talked, visited, skated, played hockey, played ball, played cards and board games and went for walks in the country. In other words they communicated and did things – with each other. And they even read books and newspapers. Then came television.

The early days of television were the best for a wide variety of reasons. There was no debate about what to watch and no need for a remote control; you had one snowy channel in living black and white. There were two choices: to watch TV or not! It was patriotic too. The daily programming started with O *Canada* every morning and ended with *God Save the Queen* every night.

By 1953, for Queen Elizabeth's coronation, CBC's programming increased to thirty hours a week. The rest of the time we could watch a snowy screen and listen to a hissing sound, or just before regular programming started we could watch the test pattern accompanied by a high pitched whine. We stared, we watched, and we were fascinated, even mesmerized.

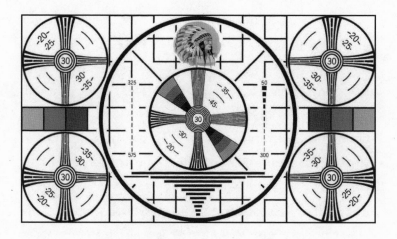

Now we get more than a million hours of programming each day on thousands of channels in living colour, in high definition, in every language known to man, beamed in by satellite signals from all parts of the globe, yet we turn on our 60 inch flat screen digital LED TV and lament that there is "nothing to watch".

By the time we got our first TV – a black and white Zenith 21 inch - at home in the Kuroki Hotel in 1958, CKOS-TV in Yorkton came on the air, and being only about sixty miles to the transmitter from Kuroki, brought a reasonable television signal most of the time. As well, by 1958 broadcasting hours had increased, starting in mid morning and lasting until after midnight on the weekends.

Others in Kuroki were on the cusp of technology with the first television set in town being purchased in 1955 by the Kanigans who owned Kuroki Café. The nearest TV transmitter was near Regina, some 120 miles away as the crow flies. Obtaining any kind of a signal was somewhat of a miracle - even with an antenna mast higher that the local Saskatchewan Wheat Pool grain elevator and stabilizing guy wires attached to anything secure within two hundred yards - but the Kanigans graciously invited town folks to come and have a look. Unfortunately, the perfect TV signal always came in about five minutes before you got there and again five minutes after you went home, at least that's what we were told. There were a few occasions on weekends when a few of us kids played marathon late night Monopoly at the café with our friend Billy Kanigan. The television signal late at night was so powerful we could recognize the images on the TV screen. Sometime around midnight, while buying Park Place and Boardwalk as well as collecting rent on our houses and hotels, we could watch a somewhat ghostly image of Perry Como crooning to all of North America. It was marvelous!

By late 1956 the Wilchynski Brothers Automobile Service Station and Garage had purchased a 20 inch cabinet television and installed an even higher mast and antenna than the Kanigans. On occasion their taller mast pulled in a fairly reasonable picture

from 120 miles distance. On Saturday nights Chris
Wilchyski would make the garage available to young
and old - males only, ages ten to eighty, to come in to
watch Saturday Night Wrestling after the 11:00 P.M.
nightly news. Ten to twenty of us all excitedly crowded
in; standing or sitting on stacks of automotive parts,
boxes of Havoline oil cans, wooden Coke boxes and
chairs, we enthusiastically cheered for our favorite good
guys and booed loudly at the bad guys. Long before
Stampede Wrestling or WWF there was wrestling live
from Maple Leaf Gardens with commentators Fred
Sgambati and Patrick Flanagan late Saturday nights.
The wrestling card usually included three matches and
assorted trash talk from the competitors who included
our national hero Whipper Billy Watson with his
famous sleeper hold, Gorgeous George (the big
meanie), the fictitious Soviet bad guy tag team dubbed
the Kalmakoff Brothers (Ivan and Karol) as well as the
popular midget tag team matches.

All night long emotions were at a fever pitch with
all of us young ones ooh-ing, aah-ing and marvel-
ing at the beatings being meted out by the brutes in
the ring. Never having seen anything like it, we were
completely convinced it was all **real,** no showman-
ship involved, pretty well the same as Gene Autry,
Roy Rogers and Superman. Long discussions ensued
between the seniors who tried to convince us that television wrestling was all fake and the young folks who

were absolutely certain someone would be killed in the ring every Saturday night. Exciting stuff! Then all week long we would talk about the bad guys and practise the Full Nelson and Sleeper holds on one another while scrapping on the playground at recess time. The only difference was that if someone was pinned, the winner would sit on the loser's chest and blow farts in his face. After that experience the dreaded Sleeper hold was child's play.

The early days of television brought something for everyone: The Ed Sullivan Show, Bonanza and the Plouffe Family for the whole family; wrestling, hockey and football for the guys; soap operas for the gals and Howdy Doody for the children. Even those epicureans who enjoyed the wholesome gourmet taste of corrugated cardboard were not forgotten. Frozen foods giant, Swanson launched a massive advertising campaign coining the phrase "TV dinner" so people could catch their favorite shows while enjoying the freezer burned taste of their favorite foods. I personally don't remember having had the pleasure of eating TV dinners. In our household home cooked food was the norm.

And life was great!

What Were We Thinking?

*There is an extremely thin line
between collecting and hoarding.
Others hoard; I collect.*

*Alicia, out first T.V. was great. But any of the television sets
we used back in Kuroki days would now be regarded as either
junk or antiques. The same can be said for almost all the
possessions we once had.*

When I was a kid in Kuroki I was surrounded by
antiques and collectibles. The nerds on the Big Bang
Theory would have envied me. I had huge stacks of
comic books of every description: Superman, Batman

and Robin, Archie, The Lone Ranger, Roy Rogers, Gene Autry, Mighty Mouse, Caspar the Friendly Ghost and a multitude of others I don't even remember. My friends had them too. We often traded and exchanged them. At the age of ten or eleven on weekends we occasionally had sleep-overs, or maybe I should call them comic-overs. We certainly didn't sleep much, but three or four of us would sit on the bed almost all night, visit and read comics until two, three or four o'clock in the morning until our legs were numb from squatting and our eyes were bleary from lack of sleep. Those comics, if kept in mint condition, would now be worth thousands of dollars, maybe more. What were we thinking when we read them, re-read them and traded them instead of saving them in pristine condition?

Comics were not the only collectibles we had. Money that once was, is no more. In Kuroki Hotel even at the age of nine or ten my brother Don and I were taught to operate the cash register, sell things to customers and make change. There were some interesting coins and paper money that passed through that cash register – many of them no longer in circulation. The most unique one I saw was a "Shinplaster", a piece of paper money with a face value of twenty cents. I never saved that one. At the age of nine I could never save the twenty cents to buy it. But there was a big 1918 penny, about the size of our current quarter, as well as a silver five cent piece, about half the size of our current dime, minted in 1917 that I received when making a sale in our hotel-café. Those two coins were unusual even in 1952. So, I hid them at the back of the cash register, and when my allowance day came - I got twenty-five cents a week back then - I paid the six cents retrieving the large penny and tiny five cent piece and saved them for the start of my coin collection. Over the years, other forms of currency have been eliminated. What became of our one and two dollar bills? And more recently the penny has met its demise.

Back in 1950 every coin, except the lowly penny and the nickel, was made of a semi-precious metal: silver. Each coin which passed through our hands was worth its weight in - uh - SILVER! There were real silver dollars in circulation in both Canada and the United States. Had we saved those silver coins in mint condition many of them would now be worth fifty, a hundred or more times their face value. We didn't know it, but we were sitting on a silver mine. What were we thinking when we spent all that silver instead of saving it in mint condition?

And the classic cars we drove! Everyone was driving a Volkswagen Beetle, a '56 Ford Thunderbird, a '49 Ford, a '57 Chevy or some other vintage vehicle. Some folks drove military green Willy's Jeeps, Fargo, International, Chevy or Ford trucks. A few of my friends even drove a "Tin Lizzy", the Model T Ford, a holdover from around 1923. My own first driving experience was with my dad's snazzy 1957 Chevrolet Bel Air, a favorite collector's model today. What were we thinking when we ripped around with those classic vehicles instead of saving them in mint condition?

We were rich, but didn't know it. We were suffocated by antiques and collectibles. We played with them, sat on them, listened to them, drove them, ate off them, read them and slept in them. Not all at once, but in the course of daily living we were regularly handling antiques. In Kuroki Hotel we had several unique ones which were not common to every household.

Kuroki Hotel-Café dining area with author's youngest siblings: John, Margaret and Jim.

This photo, taken by my father in about 1960, shows several valuable collectibles: the old cast-metal cash register, the metal mechanical scale for weighing bulk produce, the humidor for keeping cigars, cigarettes and tobacco moist and fresh, the glass display case for displaying chocolate bars and candies, the old rotating café-counter stools with cast metal bases and wood seats – what fun we had with those, trying to see if we could get them all spinning at the same time by starting one and then running along and spinning each of the others in turn. It was a great pastime if you had no iPad, smart phone or computer to amuse your tiny mind. Finally, one of the arrows is pointing to a hidden antique: soggy cotton cloth diapers. The disposable diaper was developed in 1947 by George M. Schroder working for the Textile Research Institute of the University of Chattanooga, Tennessee. However, even into the late 1960's and 1970's disposable diapers were rare, prohibitively costly and used only on special occasions or when traveling. The cloth diapers, used daily, allowed the liquids deposited therein to seep through the outer clothing so one often saw young children with wet pants. After being dirtied, the diapers had to be rinsed out, put into a holding receptacle called a diaper pail and kept there until wash day.

Looks like my youngest brother, John did a job in his pants. You can see the wetness on the pants, but who knows what other treasures were hidden inside that cloth diaper? What were we thinking when we disposed of that treasure instead of saving it in mint condition to be sold at some antique auction?

Besides the items I have mentioned we had 78 rpm records, elegant high fidelity record players, gigantic fancy oak wood radios containing dozens of glowing vacuum tubes powered by batteries as large a twelve-pack of beer, gas engine powered wringer washing machines and fancy solid silver plated eating utensils which required hand-polishing every month or so. We even had fancy oak foot-powered treadle sewing machines and valuable black Underwood manual type-writers decorated with exquisite gold lettering. What were we thinking when we used all these precious antiques and collectibles every day of our lives?

Most of the household items mentioned herein ended up on the scrap heap or were hauled to the local landfill. Some day archeologists and treasure hunters will scour the remains of the Kuroki garbage dump. Who knows what memorabilia and museum pieces they will unearth? If we had saved all that great stuff in mint condition we could have been guests on the "Antiques Roadshow" television program on PBS; or if we had used everything (as we did), but saved every last piece of crap because we just couldn't abandon that little chunk of our lives, we could have been the subjects of the television series entitled "Hoarders" on the Arts and Entertainment network. Either way, we'd be TV stars!

This should serve as a valuable lesson to all of us. Instead of using the new stuff we accumulate we should just keep it all unopened in its original packaging and store it forever. Some day we would be millionaires!

A Great Tradition

To go back to tradition is the first step forward. - Ghanaian Proverb

All families have their own traditions, their special ways of celebrating their favorite occasions. In the days before the era of cell phones and digital photography - the Kuroki days - on special occasions people would make an appointment at a photo studio to pose for a formal family portrait. My dad carried that tradition much farther than most people, in his own way developing traditions which helped to celebrate family life. One of his most interesting traditions and for my siblings and me, as we reflect on our growing up in the hamlet of Kuroki, Saskatchewan, one of the most nostalgic traditions Dad concocted was the practice of having a family outing every year on August 31, the anniversary of his marriage to my Mother. So, it wasn't Mom's and Dad's Wedding Anniversary. It was a family anniversary. The family outing was always the same. Dad made arrangements with the portrait photographer in Wadena, Saskatchewan, fifteen miles from our home in Kuroki, to have a family portrait taken on exactly August 31 each year. It didn't matter on what day of the week August 31 happened to fall. It could have been a Saturday, a Sunday, some holiday or it could have been in conflict with some other community event. We put aside everything else as the whole family prepared for the big event. Everyone took a bath. Then the guys slicked down their hair with Brylcreem, the gals dolled up with hair spray and make-up, then donning our Sunday best clothing we drove the fifteen miles to Wadena Photo Studios to pose for our annual family portrait.

A Sunday or a holiday falling on August 31 never deterred Dad from the photo tradition; and other circumstances or calamities never stood in his way. One such calamity involved an unfortunate accident which left our family without the use of our 1950 grey Chevy. In 1956 there was no such thing as water and sewer in the hamlet of Kuroki, but the Liquor Licensing Commission wanted to end the use of outhouses and honey pails in hotels and beer parlours, forcing Dad to go to the expense of installing a septic tank and a cesspool to hold the many gallons of sewage inevitably created by the consumption of liberal quantities of beer. Occasionally the cesspool would get close to overflowing and Dad would hire the local dray man, Hoot "Highpockets" Hunter – as some of the locals nicknamed him – to bring his dray with a 500 gallon tank, pump out the cesspool and haul the contents to some obliging farmer's field for disposal. On one particular day in late August, 1956 "Hoot" came with his honey wagon to empty the contents of the cesspool. Unfortunately, when the honey wagon was being backed into position one of the wheels hit a rut causing the huge tank to bounce and tip off the wagon. Fortunately no one was injured, but Dad's 1950 Chevy, parked in an inauspicious location, was badly damaged by the bouncing and rolling honey tank. With the Chevy scheduled to be in the auto body shop on August 31, Dad made a deal with Ed Wilchynski, the local General Motors automobile dealer, to borrow his brand new luxurious Oldsmobile Ninety-Eight to make the fifteen mile trek for our annual photo shoot.

What a ride we had that day! Dad used to speed a little with the 1950 Chevy, but the smooth ride of the big 1956 Oldsmobile Ninety-Eight caused him to not notice as the vehicle cruised down the old gravel Number Five highway at ever increasing speeds. We loved it until suddenly Dad remarked that he didn't realize he was travelling eighty miles an hour while the posted speed limit on that stretch of highway was a mere 50 m.p.h. He immediately slowed to 60 miles per hour, still slightly breaking the law, much to our chagrin - not about breaking the law, but rather about driving so slow.

The next year, in 1957 Dad took the plunge and bought a beautiful brand new sporty Chevrolet Bel Air four door sedan with a powerful V-8 engine from the Wilchynski Brothers. To this day I suspect that driving the new 1956 Oldsmobile made him think that he deserved a little luxury in his life. Turning sixteen and getting my driver's license in 1960, I was proud as a peacock when Dad broke down and let me use that beauty of a 57 Chevy.

On one other occasion we were nearly prevented from participating in our annual photo tradition as a result of another accident, this one caused by Dad himself: the pregnancy of our mother with her sixth offspring with a due date of early September 1959. My brother John was due to be born any day, and I recall my mother urging Dad to forego the annual tradition for just one year - she didn't want to look lumpy for the portrait, and no doubt she was in no mood for the event. However, at Dad's insistence that Mom looked beautiful and that her condition would make the annual portrait even more memorable, off we sped to Wadena one more time, cruising along in our 57 Chevy. My youngest brother, John missed being in that photo by just nine days. He was born in the Wadena

Union Hospital on September 9, 1959 and was almost one year old for the 1960 photo.

Certain other traditions always accompanied the taking of the photos. For instance, Dad always prepared for the event by purchasing a flask of Seagram's Five Star Rye Whiskey which he carried into the photograph studio in Mother's purse.

When we arrived for our appointment the photographer was always waiting for us; so we wasted no time in squeezing into the tiny powder room to have Mom do some last minute primping, Dad straightening his tie for the umpteenth time and have them both make a final effort at taming some rooster tail on the head of me or one of my siblings. With much squirming and fidgeting from the younger family members, and even some outright bawling if there was a new baby in the group, eventually we completed the posing and picture taking. Then the fun began. Dad retrieved the flask from Mom's purse, and the photographer and he (and sometimes Mom) had few quick snorts to celebrate yet another wedding anniversary. For me it was a special time when I reached the age of fourteen, being deemed to be old enough to share in the libations. Each of my brothers and sisters felt the same when they reached that special age. We were still not "legal" but Dad's philosophy was always to train us to consume alcohol in moderation. So better start the training early!

The next part of the day was even better. Wadena was and still is a town of only about 1500 people. There were no fast food places in town; McDonald's was unknown to us and dining out anywhere was a rarity. But on August 31 every year we dined out. Maybe "dined" is the wrong word. We ate at the local Chinese cafe, a fixture in most prairie small towns in the 1950's and 60's. But we considered it dining. We could order anything we wanted from the menu. Dad was treating. I was always a carnivore and every year I ordered the same thing – a hamburger sandwich with fried onions. To my recollection no one used hamburger buns in those days, particularly in Wadena. My hamburger sandwich was a handsome handmade freshly fried all beef patty about a quarter inch thick, large enough to cover a big slice of delicious Wadena Bakery white bread, topped with greasy fried onions and covered with another slice of white bread. I always had it with fries, freshly made ‑ no one used frozen fries in those days ‑ and gobs of Heinz ketchup. I washed it all down with an absolutely amazing freshly made milkshake, either vanilla or banana. It was a feast and I was DINING!

Interestingly, we were eating at the Chinese cafe but I cannot recall any of us ever ordering Chinese food, until perhaps the 1960's when our palates became slightly more adventurous.

After dining out we travelled the fifteen miles back to Kuroki and each fell into our individual routines, or if Dad didn't have to work that day we might have friends or relatives over for a visit, entertaining ourselves with some canasta card playing along with more good food and drink.

Remember, this was not the era of digital photography. The anniversary celebration continued on as the photographer sent his films away to the photo lab for developing, then some weeks later we would receive a large envelope in the mail with the "proofs" of all our poses. Every year we would excitedly peruse the proofs, laughing and teasing as one by one we picked out who had closed their eyes, looked away or frowned at the very moment the photographer had snapped the shutter. We all chose our favorite poses, then finally decisions were made and the framed photos were ordered, eventually received and proudly displayed for one year until the next August 31 and a replay of the whole production.

The photo tradition which was started by my Dad on August 31, 1950 continued until August 31, 1968. After that date our family was spread out over wide areas of Canada, and we could no longer gather on that particular date and in that specific location every year; however, for years to come Mom and Dad's anniversary was frequently an occasion when the extended family would gather to eat, to party, to reminisce and to take less formal family photos. In later years we needed a wide angle lens to fit all the wives, children and grandchildren into the photos. In the 1950 portrait there were only four of us; by 1968 the portrait included eleven of us – in living colour.

Granny

*This is a lifetime of "Good-byes".
We say goodbye to youth, to old
possessions, to old ideas and to old
friends. Eventually we say goodbye to
life itself. Have a good "Good-bye"!*

Alicia, one person who was not part of our formal anniversary portraits, but was an integral part of our family, was my maternal grandmother.

The person I mention as Granny in this part of my life is my mother's mother. When the name "Granny" is mentioned many individuals will conjure up the image of Granny, the feisty mother-in-law of Jed Klampett of The Beverly Hillbillies classic television fame. Not me.

For me, Granny was my maternal Grandmother, Caroline Mazurkewich (nee: Zluchowski), who at the age of eight immigrated to Canada from Galicia (Poland-Ukraine) with her parents in the year 1900. They settled on a homestead near Gimli, Manitoba where the records show that having lived the required three years in Canada on December 23, 1903 her father, Michal Zluchowski, became a naturalized British Subject. On February 27, 1908 at the tender age of sixteen Granny married John Mazurkewich*, aged 28, in a Roman Catholic ceremony at Sts. Cyril and Methodius Church, Gimli, Manitoba. Sometime thereafter the family moved to the Dobrowody district north of Rama, Saskatchewan where the records show that John Madzurkywicz* obtained a homestead land grant of 160 acres on April 12, 1913. The reason for the move is unrecorded, but there were three compelling possible motives: homestead land grants were available, some other relatives had moved there and many other Polish and Ukrainian families were settling in the Dobrowody area. It was more comfortable to have neighbours who spoke your native language. (Note: The Mazurkewich* name was spelled differently at different times depending upon the interpretation of the Anglo-Saxon scribe attempting to transcribe it phonetically.)

My siblings and I never met our maternal grandfather, John, who died in about 1925 leaving Granny with two daughters and four sons to raise on her own, which she did on the homestead until about 1948 when her own mother died. Shortly thereafter she moved in with my parents and me and my younger brother, Don. She lived with our family most of the rest of her life even when Dad sold the hotel, moved to a residence in the Post Office building and later moved to the town of Norquay, Saskatchewan.

Enough history already!

My Granny was a second Mother to me. She lived with us in Kuroki Hotel for almost as long as I can remember. It is said that the sense of smell is the most vivid of all senses with odours and fragrances staying longest in our memory. My own first memory of Granny was the very pleasant smell of garlic in her farm home some time before she moved in with our family in 1948. At the time I was probably three or four years of age, but to this day the smell of garlic evokes sensations of warmth, family, welcoming and friendship in my mind. There was a lot of garlic, but there were no vampires for miles around.

In most communities in 1950 folks were supremely hospitable, grew huge gardens and prepared gigantic, simple, home cooked meals. My Granny was no exception. She prepared fresh warm home-baked rye bread with caraway seeds, dripping with butter and homemade raspberry jam. Some of her specialties were homemade cheese, handmade fresh perogies, buckwheat cabbage rolls and borscht lovingly prepared with home grown vegetables. She also made choke-cherry wine and dandelion wine in earthenware crocks leaving them to ferment behind an old wood fired cook stove, later to be bottled and lovingly shared with family and friends on special occasions – there were loads of special occasions.

In the 1950's Granny worked alongside my Mom meeting and greeting guests in our hotel, preparing and serving food as well as doing laundry and washing dishes. While we all lived in Kuroki Hotel until 1962 everybody called her "Granny": her friends, the bartender, the patrons, my parents, and all townspeople who knew her. She was everybody's Granny and loved by all.

Granny's first language was Polish, but she was fluent in Ukrainian as well as broken English. I and my teen and pre-teen siblings often gently teased her and giggled about her pronunciation of some English words and expressions. For her, peanut butter was "penis butter" and apologize was "apple-jize". When something strange or unusual happened she would say, "Sometimes happens like that."

Kind and friendly to all, Granny was a hard working, devout Roman Catholic praying the rosary daily and attending Mass on weekdays as well as on Sundays. If she is not in Heaven it is likely that not many of the rest of us will make it.

Granny lived with my parents until she died at home in Norquay, Saskatchewan on February 14, 1977 and a few days later the church was filled for her funeral. Her grandson and my cousin, Reverend Father Rudy Nowakowski officiated at her funeral giving a beautiful homily paying tribute to a person we all loved. I had cried a few times in my life prior to that funeral and I have cried since, but at Granny's funeral was the first time I really bawled my head off.

Funerals in small towns and rural areas, as well as being occasions for mourning, were – and still are – occasions for gathering, visiting and reminiscing. We might be mourning, but we still need good food to help us through some sad times. In fact, immediately after every funeral service what happens? Everyone who attends is invited to eat and to drink. The human family needs food for sustenance, but even more important we need the companionship, fellowship and support that come from sharing food during celebrations of life and death.

Food For Thought

For each new morning with its light,
For rest and shelter of the night,
For health and food, for love and friends,
For everything Thy goodness sends.
- Ralph Waldo Emerson

Our ancestors were hunters and gatherers. They spent ninety percent of their waking hours in search of food or drink. Finding it was often a challenge and always a necessity. Many of our third world brethren in parts of Africa, India and Asia continue with the never ending struggle of finding enough food to eat and fresh water to drink. Most mothers with their constant commenting reminded us of these facts daily. "There are starving children in India. Eat your vegetables. Clean up your plate. Your eyes are bigger than your stomach. Save room for dessert. Don't eat that now; you'll spoil your appetite for supper. Finish your meal. No desserts for you until you finish your broccoli!" As far as I knew, in the early 1950's in Kuroki people had enough to eat, but the droughts, dust bowls and severe depression of the dirty thirties remained in the minds of many older citizens. Moreover, memories of Second World War food rationing still haunted anyone over twenty years of age. People tended to respect food; they tried not to waste.

Most folks, including my parents, raised much of their own food by growing huge gardens, and some by raising chickens, pigs and even a milk cow or goat. And almost every conceivable part of every garden plant was used in some way. At harvest time some inedible parts were simply buried, becoming compost for the next growing season. However, those farmers and small town folks who had chicken pens or pig sties simply threw the tops of many root crops into these enclosures to become food for the animals. After meals the left-overs were saved for a snack, for another meal or fed to the family dog or cat. Commercially prepared pet food was a rarity; in the 1950's dogs and cats ate people food. If after the meal there were still remaining scraps, they were thrown into a slop pail to be carried out to the chickens or pigs which greedily devoured them. The people who didn't have chickens or pigs dug a hole in the garden and dumped the slop pail there once a day. The scraps became fertilizer for next year's garden vegetables.

Gardening was a family affair. Everyone planted, watered, and weeded while swatting mosquitoes all spring and summer. We children helped, complaining the whole time that we were too hot, too cold, too mosquito harassed or that we were missing the impromptu pick-up ball game on the school grounds. Then, in autumn we all participated in a bountiful harvest. But the work wasn't over, particularly for the women. Pickling cucumbers and relish, canning fruits and vegetables and preserving cabbages as sauerkraut kept women working well into the night when the harvest was done.

In Kuroki in the 1950's many people baked their own bread. My Granny and my Mother did so occasionally, but being in the hotel business they often didn't have the time to spend baking bread, a rather labor intensive activity. Instead, once a week the Canora Bakery truck came to town and dropped off a supply of bread for our own use and to sell to customers for ten cents a loaf. On the other hand, my Aunt Elsie who lived just a block away from our hotel, baked bread every week. Monday was always laundry day, and Thursday was always bread baking day. Winter and summer, spring and fall, on Thursdays she baked enough bread on her gleaming wood-fired cook stove to last until the following Thursday. In the cooler months she not only baked, but also heated the house in conjunction with her culinary labors. But in the heat of the summer she started her baking tasks early in the morning, opening up the doors and windows to try to keep the kitchen from reaching 110 Fahrenheit degrees or more of unbearable heat as she sweated in the kitchen - mixing, kneading, stoking the fire and baking all day. For the evening meal the family was rewarded with the sight, aroma and mouth-watering taste of a dozen or more large golden loaves set to cool on long tables in the veranda. On Thursdays I considered it a special treat to visit there just to enjoy the sights and the sounds and to inhale the intoxicating fragrances emanating from her kitchen.

I previously mentioned that my Granny had a limited grasp of the English language, but she was an avid reader – of recipe books. My Mother as well as my Granny kept a stack of recipe books on one corner of the kitchen counter at all times. Whenever they had a few spare minutes they would read and re-read those books; then they would put their theory into practice by preparing awesome meals and decadent desserts. I once saw a sign in a restaurant: "Never trust a skinny cook". On that basis, if my Mother and my Granny were alive I hope they would not be offended if I called them trustworthy. However, by that measure I observed many women (and men) in Kuroki evidently even more trustworthy than my own family members.

For most of us in North America and Europe there is abundant food; in fact, around the whole world we North Americans are known for our fat asses. We are also known for the amount of food we now waste. Rather than searching for food most of our waking lives we are surrounded by it, bombarded by advertising for it and endlessly gorging on it.

Maybe it's genetic or maybe it's a cultural or social holdover from the days of scarcity, but most of us still seem to spend ninety percent of our waking lives on the topic of food. Many families are like the one in which I was raised, the one into which I married and the one into which most of us were born. We are obsessed with food. We love it. We eat; we plan to eat; we talk about food; we buy food; we eat out; we dine in; we search for and exchange recipes; we shop for food. We often do two or three of these activities at once, almost daily talking about what to have for lunch while we are eating breakfast and planning what to have for dinner while we are eating lunch. It is a never ending cycle. Multi-tasking with food is routine.

Our family loves good simple home prepared food from almost every nation and culture of the world. As I mentioned earlier, we Sliva's are of Polish-Ukrainian heritage – at least that's what we've been told. My own suspicions are that if we checked our ancestry back far enough we would have twenty or so different nationalities in our family tree. That has to be the case. We seem to enjoy food from almost every nation on the face of the earth; some we sample at a variety of ethnic family restaurants, but the ethnic foods we enjoy most are the ones we prepare from scratch right in our own kitchen. Our family loves food and drink and hospitality. Eating and drinking are necessities of life; eating and drinking with friends is the spice of life. There is absolute glee, even ecstasy, at the thought of good food or drink. My brother Jim has epitomized this feeling for over fifty years as evidenced by these two photos.

L to R: Karen Gotto, Margaret Sliva, Jim Sliva, Ray Gotto

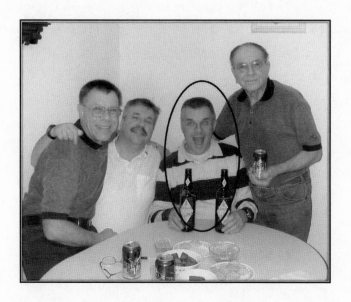

L to R: Gerald, John, Jim and Mike Sliva

The first photo was taken in 1959 when Jim was three years old. Apparently he loves cake. The second one was taken in 2003 when he was forty-seven years old. He has trouble hiding his feelings about Gilbey's Lemon Gin Collins. Put good food or drink in front of him today and his expression will be the same. We love it! We love Jim! Occasionally the rest of us have similar grins when we share a sip of gin. Then we sit and visit, tell tall tales, thank God for our blessings of life, food, friends and family; and we reminisce about the good old days.

Note to my readers: at this point in my story telling I had planned to include a few ethnic recipes, but my very helpful and wise editors advised me that recipes would interrupt the flow of my narrative. Those readers who are interested in great traditional Polish-Ukrainian ethnic recipes, like my Granny prepared, will find these in the "Recipe" section at the end of my storytelling.

Dear Old Pub

T'was a dear old pub, Kuroki pub
Where you could drink all you wanted but not
have grub
A glass of beer for just ten cents
No Indians* or women; just white gents.

In these pages, Alicia, I have often mentioned Kuroki Hotel which was my home for many years. Perhaps it is now time to tell you the gory details, the nitty-gritty of life in that hotel.

Owning a small town hotel and pub was and still is the dream of many a sentimental old fool. Some view the pub as the nucleus of a small community, a home away from home for weary travelers, and a gathering place for the healthy exchange of ideas and opinions as well as a refuge from the cares of the daily grind. For some patrons that may be so, but I saw a different side of it. My parents, the hotel owners (and also Granny) were practically tied to the enterprise. They often worked fourteen to eighteen hour days, sometimes seven days a week cooking, cleaning, serving food and beverages, entertaining and catering to the needs and desires of their customers. It was a lot like the dream of owning a fly-in fishing camp because you love fishing. When your dream materializes it turns into a nightmare. You do all the work from dawn till dusk while your customers do all the fishing.

Most of my formative years from the ages of four to seventeen were spent living, eating, sleeping, playing and praying in Kuroki Hotel. When compared to the licensed establishments of today the Kuroki beer parlour and all others like it in Saskatchewan in 1950 were primitive, restrictive, sexist and racist:

- Women were not allowed

- First Nations individuals were not allowed

- Beer parlours could not serve food

- To ensure men went home to eat, beer parlours closed at supper time

- Only beer - no wine or spirits were served

- Beer parlours were closed on Sundays and election days

- To take beer home you had to complete and sign an "Off Sale" slip

Almost everyone smoked – often "roll-your-owns"

In 1950 there was no indoor toilet in the Kuroki Beer Parlour. Men had to go out back to the outhouse to defecate, but for urination they could use a small adjoining room which contained a "honey pail" which the bartender had to haul to the outhouse daily to discard its contents – a task he relished every morning.

For my youthful curiosity the beer parlour was a constant source of amusement, wonder and sometimes dismay and fright. By the time I was fourteen Dad would invite me into the beer parlour on a Saturday morning to help clean up the place; then he would invite me to sit down and have a beer with him and the bartender, Axel Lindgren, before the pub opened for business. I was grown up! I could hardly wait till I turned twenty-one and could imbibe legally – all that beer right under my bedroom. No such luck! Dad must have had the foresight to realize that with his two older sons reaching drinking age within a few years he had better get out of the hotel business before we drank up all the profits. So, to much wailing and gnashing of teeth from my brother Don and me, he sold the place while the getting out was good.

Before Dad sold the building and our dream alcohol stash, we had plenty of extra-curricular entertainment emanating from that beer parlour. There were sporadic arguments, occasionally developing into full-blown fist fights out in the streets. There were women waiting for hours in their '49 Fords or old Fargo half-tons for their husbands to finally stagger out at supper time or closing time which was 11:00 P.M. There were women who came to the side door to complete and sign an "Off Sale" slip and take beer home with them. It was not illegal for them to drink; they just couldn't enter the beer parlour.

Growing up in Kuroki Hotel exposed me to politics in the raw. The heated political discussions in the beer parlour fueled by liberal (no pun intended) quantities of beer tended to exacerbate political rifts which occasionally spilled out onto the street or into the hotel café-dining room for curious little ears to overhear. I didn't see any fist fights over politics but I certainly heard some loud voices. Occasionally my father would get involved in some of these heated discussions, but to his credit I would hear him discuss issues and propose solutions rather than providing blind partisan support to just one political party. I often heard him give credit to one party for its stand on an issue, but then criticize that same party for its "stupidity" on another issue.

Saskatchewan and indeed all of the prairies were - and still are - a hotbed of political controversy. There was the Social Credit Party with its Funny Money financial and monetary theories, the Reform Party which promised to reform Ottawa – good luck with that – the CCF Party which later became the NDP with Tommy Douglas, the father of our Canadian Medicare System and the era of Ross Thatcher, a former CCF'er turned Liberal, who became Tommy Douglas' bitter opponent over Crown Corporations and socialized medicine. The experience of being raised in that milieu caused me to look askance at what political leaders say after I observe what they do. The attitude I have toward politics was formed from hearing my dad, after relieving one of the bartenders for a few hours, come back from the beer parlour to tell us some of the mindless alcohol fueled political drivel he had heard that day. It often went something like this:

"Clarence, why do you support the Wing Nut Party of Canada?"

"My Daddy voted Wing Nut Party (WNP) and his Daddy before him voted WNP. The WNP is the only party that has a sensible economic and social plan and the WNP tells us so. I will never vote for any party but the WNP. The other parties are to be feared because they will bring economic ruin to Canada. I'm certain of that."

* "Indian" was the politically correct terminology in 1950.

Exercising Your Franchise

Just because you do not take an interest in politics doesn't mean politics won't take an interest in you! - Pericles (430 B.C.)

When I was a kid in the 1950's, Election Day was a huge event in Kuroki. Everything else would shut down, including my Dad's beer parlour. Both sides of the street in front of the polling station would be lined with horses, cars, trucks and people. Everyone - well, almost everyone - would get out and vote. One of the sad facts of life is that today some people don't think it is worth their time to analyze their choices and to participate in the democratic process. They don't vote. We don't always know the reason why. Perhaps they are disgusted with political partisanship. Maybe they just aren't interested in politics. Whatever the reason, for a democracy to work effectively it is essential that as many people as possible get involved, learn the issues, then get out and vote.

In the 1950's and 1960's the percentage of registered voters who actually cast ballots averaged in the 75 percent range. However, in all elections since the year 2000 the percentage of registered voters who actually exercised their franchise has averaged closer to 60 percent. In the 2011 Federal General Election Canada's voter turnout rate was a meagre 61.4 per cent according to Elections Canada. Almost 40% of eligible voters didn't vote. That means 60% of us are left to decide the fate of the country.

I wondered why so many eligible voters failed to turn up at the polls so I conducted a scientific poll of non-voters to determine their reasons for not voting. The results, which are accurate to within plus or minus 5 percentage points nineteen times out of twenty, are as follows:

- 1% wanted to vote for the Wing Nut Party, but it didn't field a candidate.

- 2% said they were watching a Red Green marathon on TV.

- 4% had diarrhea and were afraid they might mistake the voting booth for an outhouse.

- 6% turned up at the polls a day late. The election was over.

- 12% said that they didn't vote because their spouse neutralizes their ballot by voting for another party.

- 14% thought none of the possible candidates was worth voting for.

- 61% got a robo-call telling them their polling station was in Kuroki, Saskatchewan three miles South of Tryhuba's* barn.

On CBC's web page one astute voter commented:

"In one the most important elections of my lifetime, almost 40% of Canadians cannot get off their arses and get to the ballot box. Pathetic - those 40% don't deserve to live in this great country.

Under capitalism man exploits man; under socialism the reverse is true. - Polish Proverb

*Tryhuba's Barn and its relationship to Kuroki: Being raised in the small but vibrant community of Kuroki, whenever people left Kuroki district to travel or to relocate for employment they spoke fondly of the "home town" to their new friends and acquaintances. When they mentioned "Kuroki", most people had never heard of the place so their obvious question was, "Where in hell is Kuroki?" To that question it became common practice for people raised in and around Kuroki to reply, "Three miles south of Tryhuba's barn." On pages 256 and 257 of this book I have included maps which show Kuroki in relation to the rest of the world. Sorry, I did not include Tryhuba's barn on the map.

Part Two

Kuroki, Buckhorn Bay and Beyond

You've Got Mail

Gratitude is the memory of the heart. - French Proverb

Besides owning the Kuroki Hotel my dad became postmaster in 1950. My uncle Mike and my dad, partners in the hotel enterprise, must have realized they would quickly become bankrupt had they tried to make a living selling beer at ten cents a glass and renting rooms to weary travellers for seven dollars a night. So Uncle Mike sought his fortune by becoming a gold miner in Uranium City in Northern Saskatchewan, and Dad took a job as postmaster while continuing to manage the hotel. He hired a bartender to sling the beer while my Mother and Granny handled the hotel-café and room rentals. Each evening, after working all day in the

Post Office, Dad would relieve the bartender, do the books and help with other tasks around the hotel.

The Post Office job was certainly no gold mine for Dad. I have in my possession the faded, yellowed, tattered letter Dad received from the Post Office Department in Ottawa in October, 1950 when he was first offered the Postmaster position. In summary, the letter said he would receive $1700.00 per year (about $142 a month). To earn that huge sum of money Dad had to provide the building to house the Post Office, do all the postal work for six days each week – Post Offices were open on Saturdays back then - perform all janitorial services, supply heat for the place in winter and pay for all utilities. In addition, he had to travel to the train station to meet the CNR passenger train twice a day to dispatch outgoing mail and retrieve incoming mail from the designated Royal Mail process-ing car - the name "Canada Post" was not used until the late 1960's. Then, immediately after receiving the incoming mail from the train Dad had to hurry back to the Post Office to sort the "Royal" mail.

For many townsfolk, twice a day when the CNR train chugged into town, the Post Office was a gather-ing place. People would eagerly assemble in the Post Office waiting room near the old-fashioned combina-tion lock mail boxes, visiting, gossiping and resting while they waited for the mail to be sorted. It was real mail! Once upon a time people sent and received real mail - authentic - handwritten - paper - personal - with a postage stamp - hand sorted by Royal Mail employees, lovingly created and dispatched by the originator and fondly read and cherished by the recipient.

Have you cherished your email recently? I'm lucky and get a warm glow all over when I think of all the people out there who love me. I personally receive fifty or more messages daily with great news and terrific offers in every one of them. Just this morning I received a personal email from a Nigerian prince trusting me to assist in the distribution of his fortune to charity, promising to bestow me with untold wealth for my trouble. Unfortunately, I really can't spare the time to respond to him because I am extremely busy corresponding with the National Online Lottery preparing to claim the huge prize I won according to the following notification:

FINAL WINNING NOTIFICATION:

Dear Lucky Winner,

RE: BONUS LOTTERY PROMOTION PRIZE AWARDS WINNING NOTIFICATION

We are pleased to notify you the Draw (#1944) of the NATIONAL LOTTERY, Online Sweepstakes International Lottery Program held on Saturday, 9th August, 2014. Participants were selected through a computer ballot system drawn from a pool of over

25,000 names of distinguished professionals drawn from Europe, America, Asia, Australia, New Zealand, Middle-East, parts of Africa, and North & South America as part of our international promotions program conducted annually to encourage prospective overseas entries. We hope with part of your prize awards, you will take part in our subsequent lottery jackpots. The result of our computer draw (#1944) which took place on Saturday, 9th August, 2014 selected email address attached to an e-ticket number 56475600545 188 with Serial number (5627635368/10) drew the lucky numbers: 16 36 40 43 45 47 (bonus no. 10), which subsequently won you the lottery in the 1st category to the sum of £7,087,472 (Seven Million and eighty-seven thousand, four hundred and seventy-two British Pounds Sterling).

Someone said that money can't buy happiness or love, but I also regularly receive loving personal offers from beautiful women inviting me into the privacy of their bedroom via their webcams. Then, too numerous to mention are the personal invitations for me to "Date Hot Russian Women". Just a few minutes ago I got an email entitled "Svetlana wants to chat with you now." You can't get more personal than that. Maybe it's just a family thing; maybe we're both loveable people. Cecilia has received a few personal offers in her in-basket too. Just yesterday she got a generous money saving offer for a potion guaranteed to enlarge her penis. She made the effort at making sure I didn't feel left out so she "personally" forwarded it to me. Is she trying to tell me something?

YOU'VE GOT MAIL!

"Bull fecal matter!" some people say. "I've got spam, tweets, twitters, texts, junk email, garbage and a multitude of miscellaneous solicitations in my email inbox. Semi-occasionally there will appear a cartoon or joke which hasn't been circulated in the past ten years. Please don't try to legitimatize it by referring to it as mail. The closest thing I've received resembling a personal email is a surreptitious selfie of some deranged secret admirer's private parts."

Anyone over fifty having any friends or relatives probably remembers a day when they sent handwritten notes and received real mail which was read and reread, treasured, stored in a shoebox, occasionally retrieved and read again. We've lost a treasure. We certainly are not deficient in the quantity of messages sent and received. If we measure success by volume we are the most communicative beings in the history of this planet.

When is the last time you put your heart and your soul into a real handwritten message to a close friend or a loved one?

Perhaps therein lies the reason for our shallow adulation and ceaseless tracking of every movement (pun intended) of certain celebrities. We are starved for human contact, real human contact - a kind word, a touch, a smile, being noticed, being appreciated; so we make up for it by sending and receiving endless texts, tweets, twitters, Facebook posts and checking our inbox every few minutes hoping someone somewhere cares that we exist. We aren't communicating with people, so we communicate with our technologies hoping they will fill that bottomless void in our psyches. The trendy observation in the 21st century is a group of people having coffee together at Tim Horton's, sitting at the same table yet each alone in their smart phone worlds.

To put a stop to all this mindless drivel I will be taking two initiatives. First, as soon as I am finished responding to the Nigerian Prince, the National Online Lottery, Svetlana and the dozens of other gen- erous offers I intend to develop a smart phone App called "HOOT". When you receive a communication you regard as garbage or offensive you simply push the "HOOT" button on your smart phone. That will immediately delete the offending communication simultaneously sending the originator the message that you don't give a "HOOT" for what you received from them.

Second, instead of complaining about the imperson- ality of our modern communications I'd like to bring back an old tradition – something from the 1950's and 1960's - the love letter. Here is my open love letter to my wife, Cecilia:

October 3, 2014

My Dear Cecilia,

Remember when we started?

It was a warm Friday evening in August, 1961.

In Saskatchewan, one small town or another held a dance either Friday or Saturday night every weekend from May until October. This one happened to be in your home town, Rama. My buddy, George, was in love with Katrina, whom he hardly knew. Katrina lived in Rama; so we travelled the twenty-two miles from Kuroki to Rama to attend the Friday night dance in anticipation of George happening to run into Katrina there and getting to know her better. It was crowded, smoky and noisy as all dances were in the early 1960's. White lightning and beer were consumed in back alleys and '57 Chevys outside the dance hall. Inside the hall older married men danced with their wives and some of the pretty young women while the teenage boys together with the shy middle aged bachelors formed the traditional stag line at the back of the dance hall. They ogled the teenage girls dancing together, whirling to the polka music and wished they had the nerve to go and ask one of them to dance without being rejected and having to make the long trek back to the stag line, head hung in humiliation. I wasn't much of a dancer. Having a raging case of acne did very little for my self-confidence when interacting with the fairer sex. I may have danced one or two dances, maybe not, depending upon whether I had taken a few sips of bravery juice. The dance was generally unremarkable for me until later that evening when George, who had located his beloved Katrina, approached me saying that one of Katrina's friends wanted to go home. Being very nervous of the stray dogs roaming the streets at night Katrina's friend had asked a group of her friends to walk her home, and did I want to come with them. I said yes. It was the early 1960's, and there were plenty of stray dogs, and people walked in those days.

So, six or seven teenage boys and girls, joking, laughing and making small talk began the short three block walk from the dance hall to your parents' home. Suddenly, after walking only a block or so your friends decided they wanted to go back to the dance leaving you to walk the rest of the way home yourself, trekking completely alone through the dangerous territory of the stray dogs. Chivalry was not completely dead. I offered to walk you all the way home while all the others returned to the dance. As we strolled along in the brilliant August moonlight we introduced ourselves and became acquainted. Walking two blocks doesn't take forever, and before I knew it you could have completely disappeared from my life. But that didn't happen.

In a few minutes we were at your house, the lights were out and I imagine your parents were fast asleep. Your Mother was a tremendous gardener and the cool night air was filled with the intoxicating fragrance of petunias and evening phlox in the flower beds surrounding the house. As we stood saying goodbye you asked me if I wanted to sit on the brick edging of the flower bed on the South side of your parents' house and visit a while. No pretty girl had ever made an offer like that to me until that night so we sat close to one another, visiting and talking, with me being too nervous to make a move. After ten or fifteen minutes I thought it was time to go, got up to say goodbye and you said the words I'll never forget, " Do you want to stay and smooch* a little?"

We smooched a little and you told me you liked my hair. Amazing!

So, there was the August moon, and the twinkling stars, and the fragrant flowers, and the coyotes howling in the distance, and the stray dogs answering, and there was you, and there was me. That was the start of fifty-some years.

In the past fifty-three years we've come through a lot together, some fun, some tears and an abundance of memories: riverbank walks in Saskatoon; date nights with movies, garlic sausage and grape juice; dances, parties, our wedding on October 3, 1964, miscarriages, our son, our daughter-in-law, our precious granddaughter, our homes, our jobs, our friends, our relatives, our retirement and everything in between.

You know the story so I won't repeat it all, but I want you to know that I love you more each day. We are different, but we're the same.

Only a few weeks ago we were watching an episode of *Family Feud* and one of the survey questions they asked one hundred women was what their husbands did NOT do for them. The number one answer was, "Thank them for what they do." Husbands DO NOT thank their wives for what they do! And I immediately thought that I thank you for what you do, but then I thought again and I realized that I rarely thank you for what you do. A long time ago I read, or someone told me, that you should tell your spouse every day that you love her (him). I have tried to do that, and when I say I love you I think it means I appreciate you, and I thank you for all you do. But you might not understand it that way, so right now I want to say, "Thank you, Cecilia, for all you do for me."

To be specific I want to list the top ten things I'd like to thank you for:

Number ten: Thank you for sticking with me through good times and bad, in sickness and in health through fifty years of marriage.

Number nine: Thank you for walking with me. Our first time together I walked you home, and I guess we've walked thousands of miles together during our lifetime. I love you for it, and I thank you for it.

Number eight: Thank you for holding my hand, whenever and wherever you do it.

Number seven: Thank you for having our son and being a loving mother.

Number six: Thank you for washing my clothes, even my stinky shorts and socks.

Number five: Thank you for making the best borscht in existence, as well as the perogies, cabbage rolls and the multitude of other good things you prepare for me and our friends and relatives.

Number four: Thank you for camping and fishing with me even when it was raining, snowing, blowing or mosquito-ing so bad that I could be accused of physical and mental abuse for taking you there.

Number three: Thank you for golfing with me. You are always my favorite golfing buddy.

Number two: Thank you for cooking, eating, praying with me and for loving me.

Number one: Thank you for saying, "Do you want to stay and smooch a little?" Yes, I still do.

Many years ago you suggested we attend the Worldwide Marriage Encounter together. We did and we agreed that it was an enriching experience. At that marriage encounter they told us that love is a decision not an emotion. I think they were wrong. It is both. In my mind I have made the decision to love you, but in my heart I feel the emotion of love for you.

I love you, and I thank you for your love toward me.

Love and gratitude,

Your husband,

Gerry

In conclusion, for those who can't tear themselves away from their smart phones long enough to write a love letter to someone they care for, I will be developing an App entitled, "Sure I love you, but until someone rips this phone out of my cold, dead hands I will not have the *time or inclination to tell you so."* It will be a very simple App. The user will simply press the "love" button and the App will immediately send a generic love letter to the intended recipient.

*NOTE: Cecilia vociferously insists that she never asked any guy if he wanted to stay and smooch a little. That's the wonder of aging and of eyewitness reports. No two individuals at the scene of the crime ever hear or see the same activity. It is the same with most things in life. It is rare that any two people will see eye to eye on everything. But sometimes it doesn't matter who remembers the real facts. By tolerating our differences for the last fifty years Cecilia and I have created some beautiful memories. Sometimes our recollections are even in synchronicity.

For instance, we both agree on the incidents which occurred in this next story starring two of my Uncles, both of whom were named Joe. The first Uncle Joe is the same fellow we visited the day I created a minor disaster by peeing in an Orange Crush bottle.

Joe One and Joe Two

Too much of anything is bad, but too much good whiskey is barely enough. - Mark Twain

In the early part of the twentieth century and even on into the later 1900's, the Canadian prairies and much of North America were a hotbed for the manufacture and sale of illicit home distilled products commonly referred to as home brew, white lightning, hooch, moonshine, rotgut, firewater, bootleg, mountain dew and various other colourful names. It was a thriving and sometimes essential part of the underground economy particularly during the depression years of the 1930's. Perhaps it still exists for all I know.

For a few academic years while attending the University of Saskatchewan in the early 1960's, I stayed in Saskatoon at a boarding house called Clinton

Lodge. A little old German couple by the name of Hans and Greta – we affectionately referred to them as Hansel and Gretel - ran the establishment for twenty or so university students. Hans was the quiet house husband and vegetable peeler, while Greta was the cook and public relations guru. She often chatted with the resident students and made small talk to pass the time. I shall never forget her telling us, on one occasion, how during the 1930's her father had made and marketed home brew (i.e. bootlegged). She said that they lived in the dust bowl of the prairies at that time. Cattle were dying due to lack of feed and water; crops burnt out from the wind, dust and hot sun, and there was a dearth of job prospects. Farm commodity prices tanked and most rural families were on the verge of destitution. Her father's small but illicit moonshine trade paid for a few groceries, keeping their large family from starving to death.

Producers and consumers of the liquid product invented various novel and ingenious methods of concealing their wares on their property. Under haystacks, in wood piles, under mattresses, in outhouses, in cream cans or on a rope down the well were some of the favourites. In those days many town folk and especially farmers kept a small supply around home "for medicinal purposes". This brings me again to a story about my Uncle Joe One.

Interestingly I had two Uncle Joes. One was my Dad's brother mentioned previously in my Orange Crush story; the other was my Dad's brother-in-law. Coincidentally, each of them had involvements with the RCMP, home brew and paying fines. The incidents involved weddings where besides serving legitimate store-bought alcohol it was expected, particularly at the weddings of Central Europeans, that liberal quantities of home brew would be passed around in gallon jugs with everyone sharing and drinking straight shots from the same glass. It was a tradition. It was also a tradition that the local RCMP detachments would check the local newspapers for wedding announcements and then do stake-outs and searches of several of the relatives of the wedding couple with the objective of finding the source of the illicit spirits and levying hefty fines in lieu of collecting taxes. Two or three Mounties with their Home Brew Sniffing Dog would descend on unsuspecting farmsteads, playing a game of cat and mouse searching for home brew stashes and/or stills. At other times, three or four Mounties would show up at a wedding dance and do an inspection of the spirits being served to determine if liquor laws were being followed. Simple stashes brought a small fine, larger stashes brought painful fines, but operating a still as a commercial enterprise could bring hefty fines and even jail sentences.

In 1964 Cecilia and I were getting married at St. Anthony's Church in Rama, Saskatchewan. Invitations were sent out and there were announcements in the local papers. Cecilia's Dad, being the dutiful father, purchased liberal quantities of cheer at the local liquor store and also sought out a source of the home made stuff to be served generously at the wedding dance. The night of October 3, 1964 the wedding dance hall was crowded, food was ample and delicious. The band was lively and liberal quantities of hooch were being consumed. The whole celebration came off without a hitch — we thought! It wasn't until a few weeks after the wedding that we heard that prior to the wedding the Yorkton constabulary had paid a visit to the residences of some of my relatives, including Uncle Joe, in search of potential home brew manufacturing or suppliers. It turned out that in their quest for sources of brew they turned up a few ounces of white lightning in my Aunt's kitchen cupboard in a vinegar bottle, kept expressly "for medicinal purposes". My Uncle Joe had pled guilty to possession, paid a one hundred dollar fine and kept the whole incident to himself until after the wedding so as not to unsettle my in-laws who were busily preparing for the wedding. When I talked to Uncle Joe some months later and expressed our regrets that he suffered an expense indirectly related to our wedding he simply joked about the whole matter. He certainly made us feel better about the incident.

Fast forward to the summer of 1966, two years after our wedding. We travelled a few hundred miles from Hanley, Saskatchewan where I was teaching school to Rama, Saskatchewan to visit Cecilia's parents. Not far from Rama was Uncle Joe's farm where we decided to pay a short visit one afternoon. Always hospitable, my Aunt immediately brought out the home made dill pickles and a variety of other delicious home-made finger foods while Uncle Joe commanded one of my young cousins to go out to the North-West corner of the hay stack near the barn and retrieve a Mickey of "good stuff" to celebrate our visit. Within minutes my cousin had retrieved a bottle from the cache. Uncle Joe and I sat at the kitchen table and poured straight shots of the brew and giggled as we reminisced about our wedding and how he had paid a fine for the very stuff we were at that moment enjoying. While we were visiting and making small talk my Aunt mentioned that by coincidence Uncle Joe's second cousin, who lived in the farmhouse across the dusty grid road from their house, not more than 150 yards from their kitchen window, was putting on a wedding for their son in two weeks. As we talked and drank we glanced across the road where the cousin lived in a house just barely visible through the poplar grove in their front yard. Just then we noticed some movement in the bush across the road. Two shadowy figures and a leashed German Sheppard were moving back and forth through the poplar grove in front of the cousin's house. As we carefully watched the scene unfold we quickly realized that it was two gendarmes with a home brew sniffing dog searching the premises for suspected illicit liquids for the upcoming wedding.

Coincidence, kismet, irony, poetic justice? Call it what you will. Here we were sitting and enjoying straight shots of brew while just across the road the yard was being searched for any signs of the stuff. Uncle Joe laughed nervously as he speculated out loud whether we should destroy the evidence by pouring it down the sink or by swiftly consuming what was left. It was a quick decision as he refilled our glasses, made a quick toast and we downed the volatile contents leaving us with a warm glow. Within minutes we repeated the performance; the evidence was gone and we sat there giggling nervously. Fortunately neither the white lightning sniffing German Sheppard nor the RCMP appeared at Uncle Joe's home that day, so we had a great story to tell for many years.

Central Europeans are known for their hospitality and for ensuring their guests are always treated royally. The incident involving my other Uncle Joe, Uncle Joe Two, who was my Dad's brother-in-law, gives a clear demonstration of that hospitality. This second Uncle Joe was marrying off his youngest son in the mid 1960's. My Aunt and he wanted to provide the best of food and drink for the few hundred guests who were to attend the wedding. Somehow Uncle Joe and his sources had eluded the constabulary in the weeks prior to the wedding celebration, and they breathed a sigh of relief when the big day arrived. The marriage ceremony at the church proceeded without a hitch; the dinner buffet was delicious, generously loaded with every kind of delicacy so common at Polish weddings - dainty cabbage rolls, delicious meat balls, ham, sausage, hand-made perogies, salads, potatoes, roasted chickens and all manner of desserts. The liquor flowed freely, and the band played lively polkas and beautiful old-time waltzes. The party was on. Suddenly a murmur spread among the guests. Word was out that an RCMP raid had taken place right at the dance hall while the party was in progress and that they had seized all the liquor in the hall. A Ukrainian-Polish wedding without liquor was unheard of. Everyone was devastated, except Uncle Joe. He had prepared for just such an emergency. Within twenty minutes he had brought in ample quantities of both home distilled white lightning as well as the government sanctioned liquids. How or where this was arranged was never discussed but his guests danced, drank and ate the night away in celebration of his son's wedding. In conclusion, to save Uncle Joe Two any embarrassment we never did ask him what sort of fine or penalty he incurred because of his liquor law infraction. We only know that we never had to visit him in the Slammer.

Thank you, Uncle Joe One and Uncle Joe Two. I toast your life, and I toast your hospitality.

Sophistication - Kuroki Style

*I have always thought of sophistication
as rather a feeble substitute for
decadence. - Christopher Hampton*

*In Kuroki we felt we always had the best of food and drink,
Alicia, but we were not exposed to big city sophistication.*

We always ate and drank heartily, but the closest
we came to gourmet dining was once in about 1954
when my Mother bought some shrimp as well as
some pimento stuffed green olives for party appetiz-
ers. The shrimp reminded me of some kind of ugly,
slimy worm and the olives looked like some stunted

still-green cherries. I gagged on the shrimp and spit out the olives the first time I tried them. I thought, "Give me roast beef, mashed potatoes and thick brown gravy. That's sophistication!"

It was the same when it came to cocktails. At parties or when we had guests my Dad often served and drank homemade carrot whiskey or moonshine or even chokecherry and dandelion wine. Not to save money; it was to be sophisticated. There was a rumour going around Kuroki that sophisticated people drank Scotch whiskey. I know my Dad tried it a few times and went back to the home made stuff or Rye Whiskey or Lemon Gin. Later, when I was a "sophisticated" student at the University of Saskatchewan I wanted to fit in with the sophisticated crowd but I found neat Scotch or Scotch on the rocks not to my liking. I mixed my Scotch with ginger ale or 7-Up to make it palatable. Occasionally I tried other concoctions in an attempt to develop a taste for Scotch whiskey. Someone (not mentioning any names) came up with the brilliant idea of buying canned peaches, straining out the fruit and using the sugar syrup to mix with the Scotch. Wow, that is one sweet drink! After all the experimentation to develop a taste for Scotch, someone (not mentioning any names) suggested we ought to buy some better brands of Scotch instead of the $5 a bottle stuff.

We had similar experiences with wines during our university years. Our sophisticated choice was a bubbly wine called "Baby Duck", sweet, syrupy and a good substitute for Coke, Pepsi or Orange Crush. But if we wanted something really special for a romantic evening we bought Ruffino Chianti even though we hadn't developed a taste for a decent wine. The bottle was the romantic part. It had a woven straw basket covering the bottom half of the bottle. When we finished the wine we could pop a candle into the bottle top to make a sophisticated table centre-piece for our next romantic interlude.

But back to Scotch whiskey! Over the years we have sampled some of the better brands – we're still working on becoming connoisseurs of fine whiskies. But my buddy Don knows that price does not always determine quality. He enjoys good Scotch and I enjoy it with him. Having an Engineering background, he is quite analytical when comparing different brands of Scotch. According to Don there is really only one way to test whether or not someone is a Scotch snob: the blind taste test. It is also the Scotch bullshit detector. You can't have preconceived notions of which Scotch is best – or the most sophisticated Scotch - if you don't know what Scotch you are drinking. It can be compared to the Pepsi Challenge, but it is even more involved and complex since there are more than the two beverages, Coke and Pepsi.

Whenever Don and I get together he goes through an elaborate ritual. He conducts "blind taste tests" to see which Scotch is the one we most prefer. The test is not based on age, price, colour, single malt or blend. It is based solely on taste preferences. Don gets three or four red tinted drinking glasses for each of us. Then, with some sticky tape on the bottom of each glass, he labels each glass with the brand of Scotch which the glass will contain and pours a small shot into each glass; then we leave the room while his good wife moves the glasses around in a random fashion.

Now comes the fun part. We come back into the room and sample each glass, making comments on our preferences. Between samples we cleanse our palates with a little drinking water. The results are almost always the same; Johnnie Walker Black Label is the hands-down favorite and we have sampled some thirty or more brands. Lest you think we are alcoholic souses we have not done all this at one sitting, but rather over the course of several years from time to time.

Try it sometime with what you assume to be your favorites and some of the lesser brands of whiskeys, gins, Scotches and other liquors. Wine aficionados can also benefit from some experimentation. They might be pleasantly surprised that they actually prefer less expensive wines. In fact, in controlled blind taste tests wine connoisseurs have shown a definite preference for less expensive vintages. Maybe we can all conserve our hard earned cash on our next trip to the liquor store. Because of Don's leadership in conducting blind taste tests we can not only be sophisticated; we can also save money!

In conclusion, it is interesting that although we have a favorite Scotch we continue to enjoy other brands. Humans seem to crave some variety in their palates.

Groundhog Day

The only man who makes no mistakes is the man who never does anything. Do not be afraid to make mistakes providing you do not make the same one twice. - Theodore Roosevelt

Alicia, since the last two stories were about alcohol, primarily moonshine, Scotch and wine, people could be under the mistaken impression that we spent our days and nights in alcoholic stupors. Such was not the case.

After Cecilia and I were married on October 3, 1964 we spent the winter in Saskatoon where I completed my Bachelor of Education degree and received my Class A teaching certificate at the University of Saskatchewan in the spring of 1965. Before I could start teaching that autumn we had to decide what to do for the summer, our first summer together. Although we would have liked to, we really couldn't afford to vacation all summer long so we did the next best thing. We were offered a deal by Ruth and Frank Prince who owned Buckhorn Bay, a small resort on Fishing Lake just three miles from my boyhood home in Kuroki, Saskatchewan. With that good fortune I didn't have to sever my umbilical cord to Kuroki too suddenly. We were to operate the concession stand, maintain the property, rent out and clean three cabins as well as rent out a few boats and motors for the season. It was pretty well a seven day a week job, but in 1965 the resort was still not too well developed so the activity was very laid back in May and June, becoming quite hectic on the July long weekend, then remaining moderate for most of July and August.

At the lake, we rubbed shoulders with many entertaining, eccentric and amusing people who vacationed there. Some of those people do goofy things when they are on vacation. They spend all year long sitting at a desk doing paper work, then during a one or two week vacation they imagine themselves to be seasoned outdoorsmen, fishermen, mechanics and professional athletes. That illusion leads to all sorts of hilarious, weird and wonderful, and sometimes dangerous incidents.

Anticipating a relaxing, fun-in-the-sun vacation one family of four rented a cottage and a boat from us for one week to do the normal lake activities: fishing, grilling hot dogs, burning marshmallows, swimming, and baking in the sun. Although the father of the family had rented a boat from the Buckhorn Bay resort, he had brought along his own brand new ten horsepower Evenrude Outboard Motor. Renting a boat was rather inexpensive, but he hoped to save a bundle of cash by using his own outboard motor to cruise around the lake exploring, sight-seeing and catching that elusive twenty pound monster Northern Pike.

It was mid-July with a beautiful weather forecast - clear skies, light winds and daytime temperatures in the low 80's (we were still using the Fahrenheit temperature scale back then). On the first morning of their vacation the father of the family wanted to get up in the cool of the morning, try out his new outboard motor and wet a line, testing out a few rumoured great fishing holes. I was up at 5:30 that morning to be sure his rental boat was ready to go, that he had life jackets and a supply of fuel. I steadied the boat for him as he checked his fishing gear and placed his shiny new Evenrude onto the back of the boat. Thanking me for getting up so early, he assured me that he had everything under control and that I could leave to enjoy that first early morning cup of java. I wished him a successful morning's catch and slowly made my way toward our concession stand and cottage about 100 yards from the beach and boat launch.

Making it barely half way there I suddenly heard a new outboard engine roaring into action. Turning around to watch him depart I saw him ease back on the throttle, slip the motor into gear then gun the engine for a speedy departure. Slowly the outboard motor lifted off the back of the transom into the air, the centrifugal force of the whirling propeller ripping the handle out of his grasp. Then suddenly the engine sank behind the boat and all was quiet except for some bubbling behind the boat and a dismayed, "Oh, shit!" coming from the lungs of the boat operator. In his eagerness to get out fishing on that first beautiful morning he had neglected to tighten the screws securing his new Evenrude to the transom. When he engaged the gears and opened the throttle his engine drove away without him. There he was, not thirty feet from the dock, up shit creek but at least he had a paddle.

I hurried back to the dock to be of assistance, but he hadn't travelled more than ten yards from the dock, so by the time I got there he had paddled back, red-facedly confessing that in his eagerness to try out his new outboard he had neglected to tighten the mounting screws securing the engine to the back of the boat. Fortunately, the water wasn't more than four feet deep next to the dock where his motor now lay. We knew it would be easily retrievable, so we speculated on whether it had been seriously damaged by its early morning plunge. Neither of us having any mechanical knowledge or skills, we simply surmised that since the engine was still cold when it took its dive it may not have sucked water into the cylinder block, but what did we know? I offered to help, but he insisted that he would handle it himself later in the day, when the sun had warmed the air somewhat, by putting on his bathing suit, wading into the water and recovering his motor. Securing the boat to the dock, we parted ways agreeing that he would take care of diving for his outboard and would call for my amateur assistance if he needed anything else.

Later that afternoon he approached me telling me he had easily retrieved the outboard and wondered if I had a sawhorse on which he could mount the motor so that he could remove the cowling, disconnect the spark plug wire and leave everything in the sun to thoroughly dry for a few days before trying it out again. Out on the lawn in front of the cabin sat his new outboard, partially disassembled, drying in the warm summer air. After two days the motor appeared thoroughly dry; so leaving the motor on the saw horse, he asked me for a ten gallon pail which we filled with water, submerging the water intake and propeller shaft. As a precaution- ary measure he had decided to try to start the engine on dry land before again venturing out on the high seas with a questionable motor. With understandable anxiety he pulled the starting rope, and the motor immediately sprang into action, merrily chug-chugging away. Hallelujah! It appeared the motor was none-the-worse from its early morning dive two days earlier.

Overjoyed at his good fortune and eagerly anticipating the fishing, cruising and exploring in store for him and his family, he decided to wait until later the next morning, the third day of his seven day vacation to proceed cautiously and take his family for a little spin in the bay before venturing further afield that evening to stalk the legendary mammoth Northern Pike.

To make a short story even shorter – most of us are familiar with the movie Groundhog Day in which Canadian actor Bill Murray relives the same day over and over again. Sadly it was the same for this gentleman and his family. He lifted the motor on to the back of the boat, helped his wife and family adjust their life jackets and get seated comfortably for a scenic trip around Buckhorn Bay.

Seated in front of the confection booth I suddenly heard the roar of a new outboard engine starting. Glancing around to watch the family depart I saw him ease back on the throttle, slip the motor into gear, then gun the engine for a speedy departure – you probably guessed the rest. It was déjà vu, one more time, all over again. The only difference was that this time he made it twice as far from the dock. His engine was now in ten feet of water, and his wife and children were there to hear him using expletives about his bowel movement.

Needless to say, by the time he used his diving skills and a rope to again recover his motor, spend another two days to disassemble and dry it, then reassemble it once more, his vacation was nearly over.

Happy holidays until next year!

Puppy Love

Dogs believe they are human.
Cats believe they are God.

Besides fishing, boating, camping and sunbathing on the sandy beach, some folks spent their days and nights engaging in torrid love affairs. Alicia, since your mother, Cecilia, and I were married less than a year, we spent most of our time with one another in marital bliss. Such was not the case with everyone in Kuroki or at Fishing Lake. Some young folks were looking for "action".

The hot, humid summer of '65 was the perfect time for a love affair in the sleepy little hamlet of Kuroki. When he first saw her he knew he couldn't live without her; she was his obsession, his everything, his first love: tempting, exciting and impetuous. It was a torrid romance. The slim, sexy blue-eyed blonde beauty well knew her seductive charms would enchant him, lure him, and entice him to invite her into his warm bed and eager, waiting open arms. She was a seductress above all else. My parents warned him about her; they told him not to sleep with her, that she would be nothing but trouble, but he was too young to know; he wouldn't listen. The first time she entered his bedroom he thought they would be together forever. She lived up to the tang, the spiciness of her name – Ginger, and what a beauty she was! They told him she was nothing but a bitch, a dog not worthy to sleep in his bed, but John knew better. He was head over heels in love.

My youngest brother, John, was six years old at the time, and Ginger was his dog. He loved that dog - blonde haired, beautiful and sleek, but a very misbehaved one year old pure bred Husky. Every chance he had, John played with her, and she followed him everywhere, but she had a naughty streak in her. Somehow when she saw anyone walking she was inspired to nip at their heels, an annoying habit which young John was unable to break. When my dad was in the vicinity, Ginger seemed to know who was boss and restrained herself, but otherwise she became intolerable, so he had her chained up for most of each day until John got home from school to play with her.

In Kuroki in 1965 all dogs ran loose, and Dad was loathe to chain up the high-spirited animal. Fed up with her tactics but feeling that perhaps if she had more freedom to run loose she might run off some of her excess energy and be more sedate around people, Dad asked if we would take Ginger to Fishing Lake where we were spending the summer at Buckhorn Bay, just three miles from Kuroki. It was close enough to town so that John could come almost daily to visit and play with his beloved Ginger. Somewhat skeptical of the outcome I agreed to give it a try. At Buckhorn Bay during the week there were a few fishermen, but very few swimmers, so I felt it was safe to allow Ginger some freedom to roam the nearby bushes chasing rabbits or squirrels to perhaps run off some of her surplus energy.

That worked fine from Monday through Friday, but on the weekends with more people visiting the beaches I kept Ginger on a long chain thirty or so yards from our cabin to prevent her from annoying our customers. Once, even in mid-week I received a complaint from the Red Cross swimming instructors at Saskin Beach that Ginger was pestering the children on the beach. At that point I knew I had to keep her chained up most of the time – a bad situation.

In the first few years of our marriage we were pet people. At the lake we also had a cat, a huge lazy grey female named Fluffy, but nicknamed the "Lynx" for her size and her slow, deliberate stealth. From her nose to the tip of her tail when the Lynx stretched out she was nearly a meter long. She was generally a house cat, except for her daily routine of bathroom breaks. She spent most of her day lying in the warm sun and sleeping either in front of the cottage or inside on the sofa. Stretching her ample frame onto the middle of our old green sofa she left little room for anyone else to relax there. She once told me that she owned that spot on the sofa – that neither I nor Cecilia nor Ginger could ever have it.

So there we were at the lake, falling into a sleepy summer routine of cleaning cabins, selling hot dogs, swimming, fishing, visiting with friends and relatives, feeding mounds of food to the Lynx and to Ginger as well as chaining Ginger when needed. Unfortunately,

Ginger was a fast learner, when it came to the things she wanted to learn. Early on Saturday mornings I would get up, call out to Ginger and prepare to chain her for most of the weekend. I didn't like it, but she particularly despised being restrained, and did all she could to avoid it. On one beautiful Saturday morning I called to Ginger several times, and several times she came to me, but the moment she spied the chain she bolted away. I was dealing with an animal that was out-smarting me. Almost ready to give up, as a last resort I moved the chain into the cottage entrance, deciding to lure her in with food and snap the chain on her there. I went to the fridge, procuring a fresh wiener, calling to Ginger and tempting her with the delectable morsel I waved in front of me. It was a flawless plan. Almost immediately she joyfully bounded toward me drool-ing profusely.

Unbeknownst to me I had unleashed the Hound of Hades. In my eagerness to lure the dog into the cottage I had neglected to notice the Lynx lying peacefully on the sofa in full view of the entrance. At the very moment Ginger saw the Lynx, the Lynx saw Ginger, and all hell broke loose. The wiener was no distrac-tion for Ginger as she raced past me almost knock-ing me to the floor, making a bee-line for the rapidly disappearing feline rounding the corner and heading for the bedroom where Cecilia was still fast asleep. Almost simultaneously there were canine and feline paws skidding on the old linoleum floor, then loud barking, desperate mewing and blood-curdling screaming coming from the bedroom. The Lynx, in a vain attempt to escape the charging Ginger, had jumped onto the bed on top of the very startled Cecilia, and dug her razor sharp claws through the blanket into Cecilia's legs. By the time I got to the bedroom the Lynx, Ginger and Cecilia were one furious ball of rage. It was a hilarious situation, but I dared not laugh – I was too young to die. Finally, grabbing Ginger's collar I dragged her along the floor, out the door and chained her to a tree. All the while she continued to growl and bark furiously at the hissing cat.

When I returned to the cottage the commotion had run its course, but at that point we both decided that Ginger's vacation was over – she had to leave Buckhorn Bay. She was Dad's problem once more. Dad hated to break up the budding romance between my six year old brother and the love of his life, but keeping the poor dog chained up all the time was not fair to anyone, particularly to Ginger. Dad pondered his options and decided that his best bet was to take Ginger to the Wadena Auction Mart the following Saturday to see if he might raise a few bucks from some farmer wanting a fine looking farm dog. On auction day Dad confidently paraded Ginger in front of the crowd. Alongside Dad she stood quiet and tall, a sleek handsome looking beast. It was over quickly, a couple of farmers toyed with some bidding and she sold for five dollars, not a huge sum, but Dad was happy for himself and for Ginger – she had a new home, and she would make that farmer a terrific working farm dog: alert, intelligent and capable.

Little did Dad know. Two weeks later when for some reason Dad returned to the Wadena Auction Mart he found Ginger being paraded in front of the crowd by the new owner. This time she sold for fifty cents. When the auction was over Dad approached the farmer who had purchased Ginger two weeks previous and asked him what the problem was. The farmer was not happy. Sternly, he informed Dad that in just two weeks Ginger had worn out her welcome, first by chasing his herd of milk cows around so much that they wouldn't give milk, then by breaking into the chicken pen and killing twelve of his best laying hens.

Johnnie's first love was incorrigible. Whatever became of her we do not know!

Life on a Thread

Ever since the day I came out of the womb, I've had impeccable timing. For example, I somehow managed to be born on the exact day of my birthday. And I wasn't even trying, though my mother did push me along a bit. - Jarod Kintz

Cecilia and I were married in October 1964. Then in 1965, that first whole summer of our life together, we were at Buckhorn Bay having adventures with Ginger the dog and the fellow who kept drowning his Evenrude outboard motor.

In late June of that summer Cecilia began to be plagued with nausea and vomiting. We attributed it to the water at Buckhorn Bay, but when the symptoms persisted she visited the doctor in Wadena, some fourteen miles away. He suspected that the moonlight reflecting from the water at Fishing Lake may have resulted in some romantic interludes. Attributing her illness to pregnancy and to morning sickness he administered two pregnancy tests, one of which came back positive. Turns out that little Johnnie wasn't the only one in love that summer.

Having graduated with a Bachelor of Education degree that spring, while we worked and entertained ourselves at the lake, I was applying for teaching jobs. I landed one in Hanley, Saskatchewan just forty miles south of Saskatoon where in the fall of 1965 I began my teaching career as high school teacher of English Literature and Composition primarily to grades ten and eleven.

Hanley, with a population of about five hundred real people plus dozens of mandatory dogs and cats, was another "Kuroki", just a little larger than my first Kuroki. Although the town was small, the Hanley Composite High School was quite large with fifteen school buses bringing students from a large rural population (many devout Mennonites with large families) as well as students from the Dundurn Army Camp some twenty miles away. In total there were nearly 300 students in Junior and Senior High School all eager to be educated by a greenhorn English teacher – that's me!

Hanley was a great place for our first real home: friendly, welcoming people, wide open prairie skies and just a forty-five minute drive from the metropolis of Saskatoon – the cultural centre of Canada. Unfortunately, when we first went to see the place we almost panicked. There was no housing available for rent. The large school with the large number of teachers meant that all available housing in the small town was taken. After talking with several townspeople we learned that one small house might be available. We went to have a look; it didn't take long. The only available "residence" was a two room dilapidated red brick siding shack on the eastern edge of town. It was less than 400 square feet in area renting for $20 per month. It had electricity, but no running water and no furniture or appliances. Its one modern convenience was the traditional outhouse in the back yard. Surprise! We had returned to Kuroki in 1950! Nostalgia is great, but this was ridiculous.

We had two choices: take it or leave it. In reality we felt we had no choice, so we took it hoping that by the time Cecilia was due to deliver our baby we would have found better accommodations to greet our newborn. For that first "home", from a second-hand store in Saskatoon we purchased furniture and appliances: a bed, an old electric stove, an antiquated International Harvester Refrigerator (and I thought they only made farm machinery), a small sofa and side chair, a black arborite kitchen table with four black leatherette covered chairs, four old wooden Coke boxes, one of which served as a TV stand; the others alternated as extra chairs, end tables or coffee tables as the need arose. Oh yes, we also had a high end bookcase constructed of sixteen used bricks and three new spruce boards. The total cost of the elegant furniture for our luxury home was $325.

We were slightly naïve. I had a university degree and a job as a professional high school English teacher. We thought we were going to be living high, but we received a bit of a shock when my first paycheque arrived at the end of September. After deductions for income tax, union dues and unemployment insurance premiums my cheque was $370 for one month of teaching, preparation time, assignment marking and extracurricular supervision. Less than two bucks an hour! What were we going to do with all the cash left over after we made our $90 monthly student loan payments? We were on a tight budget in Spartan surroundings. Not having running water we had to make regular weekend trips to Saskatoon to take dirty clothing to a Laundromat, do some visiting and purchase groceries for the coming week. For drinking and washing water we are forever indebted to our kind neighbours, Roy and Nell Matthews, who regularly ran a garden hose over to our house to top up a drinking water tank and a wash water reservoir.

Cecilia was ready to file for divorce, but she was trapped. I kept her barefoot, pregnant, hungry and in strange new surroundings. She was stuck with me. I was suffering from first year teaching blues while Cecilia continued to suffer from severe symptoms relating to her pregnancy and even some very early contractions threatening her with a miscarriage. This continued until November 1965 when Cecilia was nearly six months into her pregnancy as far as the doctor surmised.

Then at 2:00 A.M. one morning in late November Cecilia roused me from a deep sleep telling me that she was experiencing fairly heavy contractions and that her water had broke. This was serious. Our child was not due to arrive for at least three months; we were over forty miles from the nearest hospital, and it had been an early start to winter with freezing rain turning Highway Eleven between Hanley and St. Paul's Hospital in Saskatoon into a dangerous skating rink.

That forty mile drive to St. Paul's Hospital was one of the scariest drives of my life. For Cecilia's sake I wanted to get there as quickly as possible, but getting there in one piece was somewhat of a challenge. My old green '59 Chevy was practically floating along on the black ice of Highway Eleven as I tried to keep a steady pressure on the gas pedal and my foot off the brake to avoid going into an uncontrollable spin on that nerve-wracking trip. There were very few vehicles on the road at two in the morning. With me exceeding the speed limit, the road a sheet of ice, me in a panic and the era well before cell phones, we would have met disaster if we had hit the ditch. Our guardian angels must have guided us all the way to Saskatoon safely early that morning. But we were not at the hospital yet. We had to skate our way down 8th Street and over to St. Paul's Hospital on the West side of the city.

By the time we reached 8th Street it was almost three o'clock in the morning, and the roads were nearly deserted. In my anxious state, with Cecilia on the one hand telling me to drive carefully and on the other hand moaning in pain because of her contractions, I continued to speed down icy 8th Street ignoring red traffic lights and speed zones. All went well until we were crossing Clarence Avenue South. For some reason there were four or five vehicles waiting at that intersection ready to cross 8th Street when their traffic light turned green, but at the speed I was going compounded by the icy conditions, we were tempting fate. Suddenly the light for me turned amber, then red. I knew if I applied the brakes I would be skidding into one of the vehicles crossing my path with disastrous consequences. I took my foot off the accelerator, leaned on the horn with all my might and squeezed through the intersection honking and zigzagging my way past vehicles crossing 8th Street from the North and the South. Cecilia just about had our baby right then and there, and I came dangerously close to a monstrous bowel movement, but again we were spared. That close call forced me to reconsider my speed. We were close enough to the hospital that I felt I should obey the traffic laws and get us the rest of the way without incident. Our son had already had some brushes with death, and he wasn't born yet. No point in his dying in a traffic accident on the way to his birth!

Within minutes we were pulling up to the Emergency Entrance of St Paul's Hospital, securing a wheelchair for Cecilia and receiving almost immediate attention when I described our situation to the duty nurse at emergency. The emergency staff contacted Dr. Kost, our family physician, who immediately prescribed medication to stop the uterine contractions. When he arrived at the hospital he advised us that Cecilia would have to remain in hospital and be confined to complete bed rest to reduce the chances of an early delivery. He said that every day that the baby could remain in the womb would improve fetal lung development crucial for the baby's survival.

We had to face facts. Cecilia had to stay in the hospital. I had to go back to Hanley to prepare, administer and grade the pre-Christmas English examinations. Our son – I called him our son even though we never knew the gender – had to stay inside his Mom, at least for a while to allow his tiny lungs to develop. He might not have had fully developed lungs, but he certainly had a one track mind which seemed to be telling him to escape from that nice cozy womb to explore the cold, cruel, icy world.

Those were our lives for a few weeks. The stress was intense for all of us. Cecilia was in fairly constant discomfort and pain, the drugs suppressing the contractions but not completely eliminating them. Driving our green '59 Chevy, I visited her each day, slipping and sliding forty miles each way down that treacherous Highway Eleven which remained icy for the duration. Then I burned the midnight oil doing the work involved in teaching English to some 120 high school students. And all the while the stubborn little guy kept trying to get out of that warm restful womb. I would have loved to trade places with him. Little did he know what an icy cold, slippery, snowy world he faced if he did survive his journey outside his mother.

This hectic routine continued for all of us until the evening of Monday December 6, 1965. Then things got wild. About 7:30 that evening, as was our routine, Cecilia was lying in bed still experiencing mild contractions in spite of the medication to prevent them. She was quite sore and uncomfortable after being obliged to lie there for the previous fourteen days. I was sitting by her bedside trying to visit with her, comfort her and distract her from her seemingly endless misery when suddenly she said she felt something coming out from between her legs and she asked me call the ward nurse who took one look and called the doctor. From that moment the activity was hectic. The doctor quickly explained to Cecilia and to me that the umbilical cord was being expelled, a condition referred to as a prolapsed umbilical cord, and that an immediate emergency caesarean was necessary to have any chance of the baby's survival.

Within minutes Cecilia was in the operating room, and I was pacing and smoking in the waiting room – yes smoking was permitted there in 1965, and I was still hooked. The whole operation occurred very quickly. Cecilia was given a local anaesthetic, prepped for surgery and our baby was extracted through an incision in her abdomen all within twenty minutes. It happened so quickly that I hardly had time to be frightened and to consider the true gravity of the situation.

Within a half hour the doctor was telling me I was the father of a three pound ten ounce son who was alive, breathing with some assistance, but whose life was still hanging by a thread. He advised me that our son was in an incubator, that the next forty-eight hours were crucial in indicating whether he would survive and if he might be healthy. I asked how Cecilia was doing. He said that she had lost some blood because they had had to make a larger incision than usual. Just as they were removing our son, Cecilia had a uterine contraction which clamped over the baby's head. He said that Cecilia was receiving a blood transfusion and that they were working at suturing her incision as well as stemming her bleeding and her continuing contractions which further exacerbated the bleeding. He said he would report back to me shortly. Now I was scared! Our son's life was hanging by a thread and my young wife's situation was still precarious.

Now nicotine and caffeine were my only friends. I paced constantly, wondering what fate awaited our tiny family. It seemed like hours, but within another half hour the doctor came to the waiting room and told me I could see Cecilia, that they had stabilized her, cleaned her up and that she was resting in the recovery room. He cautioned me not to be alarmed at a spattering of blood on some of the bedding as that had not yet been attended to. She had lost a bit of blood and the transfusion was still in progress, but her bleeding seemed to have stopped. He said that I should make the visit brief because Cecilia needed as much rest as possible after her ordeal. I said a quick prayer thanking God for the work of the doctors and hospital staff as well as for Cecilia's recovery as I headed down the hallway to see her.

When I arrived Cecilia was connected to a couple IV's and a heart and blood pressure monitor. She was pale, but alert. I kissed her gently and told her I loved her. She gave me a weak smile warning me not to touch her body as she was still in pain. I stood quietly by her bed, wanting to hug her but just gently holding her hand for several minutes. The doctor had told her of our son's continuing struggle to survive, so we just remained there in silence until the doctor came and told me it was time to go. Cecilia needed to rest and to sleep. I kissed her gently, squeezed her hand and left.

My drive back to Hanley that night was filled with questions about pain, life, death and eternity as well as prayer for our small family. That night I tossed and turned wondering what fate awaited us. In the morning I phoned the school Principal advising him of our situation and asking for the day off to return to Saskatoon to be with my wife and new son.

Back at St. Paul's Hospital in Saskatoon Dr. Kost met with us to provide more details about Cecilia's prognosis and what was in store for our premature son. Dr. Kost assured us that Cecilia would be fine, that she had to remain in hospital a few weeks for observation and to ensure she had no internal bleeding, but then she could come home with me as long as she was very careful not to do any lifting of any kind and not to exert herself in any way for several weeks to ensure that her stitches did not pop causing her to bleed internally.

The life of our son, on the other hand, was still hanging in the balance. Dr. Kost advised us that children born about three months prematurely often have poorly developed lungs; furthermore, the prolapsed umbilical cord can deprive the fetus of oxygen and essential blood supply leading to possible brain damage. He felt that because of the emergency caesarean our son had a good chance and that the main issue was whether his lungs were developed sufficiently. He repeated what he had said the previous night, about the next forty-eight hours being crucial.

Then, very slowly, we went to see our son. Cecilia had been out of surgery for less than twenty-four hours and had to be carefully helped into a wheelchair. As well, she was still dragging an IV bottle around so her movements had to be slow. Unfortunately we couldn't get too close to our new son. We had to view him by peering through the large window into the ward where the preemies were kept in incubators. From a distance we saw this hairy little fellow with jet black hair and a definite Sliva nose even though he was less than 24 hours old. I knew I was the father! Both he and his incubator were hooked up to various gadgets to provide him with life support. We remained there for several minutes admiring him from a distance. It was painful to see the little guy and not be able to hold him, cuddle with him and let him hear our voices telling him that we loved him, but in 1965 that was the way things were. We were not allowed near the incubator.

When we returned to Cecilia's hospital bed we sat and decided we were going to be optimistic about our son's chances and pick a name for him. Seemed to me he looked a lot like Gregory John Sliva, so that's the name we settled on. Gregory would be formal enough if his Mother wanted to scold him, yet Greg would be short enough to be casual and friendly most of the time.

The next month seemed to drag on forever with my driving daily from home to the hospital and back again. Both Cecilia and Greg, after the initial scare they gave me, continued to improve in health and strength. Ten days after the caesarean, Cecilia came home in a flood of tears at having to leave her new son in the hospital. Greg gained weight quickly. After some initial weight loss he almost doubled in weight to about six pounds by early January 1966 at which time Dr. Kost advised us he was healthy enough to come home to Mom and Dad. Being first time parents our worries weren't over. Every grunt, whimper and groan of the alien little being threw us into a tizzy.

Two characteristics of premature babies are that many of them have a significant amount of body hair and that they make grunting noises much of the time. Our son had both characteristics. By the time he came home with us he seemed to have lost some of the body hair, but his grunting continued for several months, so much so that I nicknamed him Gregory "Grunt" Sliva.

Since those days during the winter of 1965-66 we thank God that Greg has been a healthy, intelligent fellow. He graduated from the University of Regina with an Honors Chemistry degree, became a successful Chemist, married a successful nurse, Grace Gillis, and together in 1999 they presented us with a beautiful, intelligent granddaughter, Robyn. Greg has gained a few pounds since his initial weigh-in at three pounds, ten ounces. At times he now polishes off a beef steak about the same size as his birth weight.

Names and Labels

Any child can tell you that the sole purpose of a middle name is so he can tell when he's really in trouble. - Dennis Frakes

Alicia, when we chose your name and a name for our son, Greg, we took the task very seriously. Choosing a name for a child is such an important and difficult duty as well as quite a responsibility. One's name is the label he carries with him for his whole existence. Names and labels can be heavy burdens or a great asset worth millions or billions of dollars. For instance, you could offer Google Inc. billions of dollars for their name, but there is little chance of them selling.

In Kuroki in mid-twentieth century adults' names were divided fairly clearly along the lines of ethnicity or country of origin. There were the Scandinavians: Axel,

Elis, Nels; there were the Slavs - Polish/Ukrainian/ Russian: Joseph, Michael, Anne, Elizabeth, (mostly named after saints); there were the Germans: Günter and Wilhelm. And so on with each nationality. You could almost predict the name if you knew the national background of an individual.

Most people are somewhat judicious when choosing names for their children, trusting that the children would like their names when they got older. They do not want their children to be saddled with names that seem to be some whim of their parents. That whim should be permitted to go only so far. Occasionally judges and the courts have intervened to prevent parents from getting too stupid when naming their child. For instance, a New Zealand judge blocked the parents who tried to name their son "4Real" stating that it was unfair to the child. And in France a child was renamed by the courts after the parents dubbed the girl Nutella. In essence the court said that the name "Nutella" given to the child is the trade name of a spread, and it is contrary to the child's interest to be wearing a name which can only lead to teasing or disparaging thoughts. In the U.S.A. parents are given free rein when choosing names for their children. Professor Charles P. Gerba of the University of Arizona Department of Soil, Water and Environmental Science, who made it his life's work to study bacteria and viruses, gave one of his children, a boy, the second name "Escherichia" after the bacterium Escherichia Coli, better known to us as the E. Coli bacteria. You be the judge of that one! And the children of certain movie stars and celebrities are tagged with some rather unusual names – unique, but unusual. Are they doing it to satisfy their own need for attention? Are they trying to give their child a lesson in the school of hard knocks with the teasing they might receive? Or are they doing it for their own publicity? Each child is a unique gift from God and as such deserves a unique name, but there should be some common sense rules.

What do most parents do? They look at the family tree. Should they name their new offspring after a favorite grandparent, uncle, aunt, friend, ex-boyfriend, ex-girlfriend and the list goes on and on? They buy books on popular children's names, search the internet for suggestions, talk to one another and agonize over the decision for weeks and months. God forbid a new prince or princess is born into the Royal Family, or there is sure to be a spate of children whose parents believe they too are royalty and should be so named. They even pick possible names before the woman is pregnant in anticipation of some future joyous event. They look at first, second and third names and combinations of names which might be harmonious with the surname, over which they have little choice.

After all the time, effort and debate what name does the child receive? Larry, Don, Mary, Fred, Peter, April,

May or June! It depends what month or into what era and into what cultural, religious, ethnic or national background one is born. You won't find too many Christian children with the given name of Mohammed or Krishna. And there aren't many Moslem children named Nigel or Jesus. Michael is a great name; in fact it is my second given name. It was exceptionally popular in the first thirty years of the twentieth century. My Dad is Mike, my father-in-law is Mike, I have two uncles named Mike, and I know dozens of other Mikes. All very nice people! Not to single out the Michaels of this world, the same can be said of all the people named Joe, Mary, Larry, John, Fred, Pete, Ann, Doris or George. They are unique. Their names aren't.

We spend part of the winter in an age fifty-five plus RV park in Arizona. If you holler "Larry" anywhere in the park you'll have a dozen or more aging gentlemen in various stages of ambulatory ability or disability running, walking, hobbling, limping or golf-carting in response to your call. Or you might have no one coming. It depends whether or not they had their hearing aids turned on. Try hollering "Don" and you'll obtain an identical response from a dozen or more other guys.

There are a million people named John Smith. This leads to all sorts of problems of identity theft, mortgage loan approval, credit card issuing and roll call in elementary school.

Maybe you don't want or like your name. If your name is Kermit you will forever be associated with an adorable green frog. Maybe there's a child molester, rapist, thief or murderer with your name. Or maybe there's a president, prime minister, politician or, heaven forbid, a disreputable senator carrying your handle. Hang your head in shame. My given name is Gerald. In the early 1950's there was a cartoon character named Gerald McBoing-Boing. At a tender age I was referred to as Gerald McBoing-Boing and I was not fond of it. Then, when I was a little older, Gerald Ford became President of the U.S.A. forcing me to suffer through another round of Gerald associations.

Conversely, if you are lucky, your name might be associated with a popular actor or figure skater or with warm, loving thoughts like good home cooking. Not long ago on the Comedy Channel we saw a comedian who asserted that if you want good home cooking you have to marry a woman with the right name. If you want home baked apple pie or cake made from scratch you certainly wouldn't marry someone named Tiffany or Scarlet. If a made-from-scratch pie is high on your list of priorities for marital bliss you'll want to marry someone named Edna or Ethel.

Then there's the issue of people choosing to use their second name rather than their first name or a nickname they have been labeled with like Skip, Boo, Boy, Honey, Red, Chubby or Beanpole. Even if their given name sticks, Richard becomes Dick; Charles converts to Chuck; James becomes Jim; Joyce reverts to Jo or Joy; Christopher becomes Chris and so on.

Further problems arise with unisex names like Gerry (that's me), Jean, Morley, Bailey or Sasha leading to a gender identity crisis and rampant homosexuality.

You think your name is unique? Think again. There are far too many people having exactly the same name as you have. As evidence of this just try to register for an email address with Google or Yahoo or any of the other popular email sites using your first and last names as the first portion of the email address. You can't do it. Some dirty bastard with exactly the same name as you has already taken that email address.

I propose a solution to nip this fiasco in the bud. Under my proposal parents would have the right to choose a temporary name for their child, say to the age of sixteen or eighteen. Then when the child is ready he/she gets to apply for their unique name. We are in the digital age allowing us all to have unique names which truly identify us as individual human beings. Just as we now have to apply for a unique email address or obtain a unique license plate for our automobile we could do the same to select our one-of-a-kind name. We would have a choice: either we take the next name that comes up when we apply to the big computer in the sky, or we could use our ingenuity to create a name that no one else can have. It is our name. It should be as unique and as individual as we are. We should settle for nothing less. By the way, the one-of-a-kind name I chose for myself is golfprowannabe9416@hoot.com. My first choice was "Tarquin Fin-tim-lin-bin-whin-bim-lim-bus-stop-F'tang-F'tang-Olé-Biscuitbarrel". However, according to Wikipedia that name was already taken by a British political candidate who re-named himself after a Monty Python character.

Sorry, I think I may have been barking again. We have bigger problems than parents choosing names for their children. One of those problems is that people of certain groups are labelled as lazy, intelligent, athletic, musical, dumb, attractive or savage. The real problem with labelling is that it unfairly puts individuals of that group in a box, tends to keep them in that box, and makes it difficult for them to escape, to become individuals and to reach their full potential. I hope my next true narrative sheds some light on that issue.

Dumb Polacks and
Lazy Indians

Racist thought and action says far more about the person they come from than the person they are directed at. - Chris Crutcher, Whale Talk

Our son, Greg, is a successful Chemist and a fine father and husband. We love him dearly, but he was once a dumb Polack. That was many years ago - about 1972. Our seven year old son came home from school one day just giggling about the "Dumb Polack" jokes he had been told at school by his friends and classmates. He told his Mother a few of the jokes. Some were racist. Some were obscene. Some were even funny. Then he asked, "Mom, what's a dumb Polack?" Being of Polish heritage, she jokingly replied, "You're a dumb

Polack." Then, to our seven year old son, she went on to explain ethnicity and heritage and race, and how some people make jokes about people of other ethnic or racial backgrounds. Seems he didn't find the jokes so funny anymore.

Along similar lines, as I grew up in the small hamlet of Kuroki, there was a North American Cree Indian family that lived there in a small two room unpainted shack with a wood stove for cooking their food and heating their humble rented residence. It was unusual to have an Indian family living in town, because almost all Indians lived on Indian Reservations. This family, the *DesGeorge's consisted of the mother, Mary; the father, Charlie, and three children, Alex, Lilia and Leon. Alex was about my age and attended the same two room red brick school building that I attended until the 10th grade. Their grandfather, John DesGeorge, was a friendly grey haired gentleman who had served overseas in the Second World War. He never lived in town, but regularly came in from the reserve for a few beers at Kuroki Hotel and a visit with his son, daughter-in-law and grandchildren. The Kuroki Hotel Beer Parlour was "Men Only", no women or Indians allowed in the 1950's (The good ole days, eh?). John and Charlie received some kind of exemption to this rule. Perhaps it was because they were Métis or maybe because of John's military service. Being a little more educated and perhaps having the foresight to realize that there was no future for them on the Fishing Lake Indian Reserve, with limited success Charlie and his family tried to eke out an existence in Kuroki and provide the children with an education.

There was a lot of racism in small town Saskatchewan in the 1950's. One often heard comments from townsfolk about "lazy Indians" or "drunken Indians". There's probably still a lot of that today. Racism, the political system, the Indian Act, the Indian Reserve system and some First Nations Chiefs and Councils are holding the rank and file First Nations People hostage.

Alex DesGeorge was my friend, not a close friend, but he was a close acquaintance who lived just a softball throw away from our family. At recess time in summer we played catch and scrub softball. After school we wrestled and played cricket using discarded Texaco oil cans as wickets. In winter we played crokinole in the classroom or marbles in the school basement. Alex was not lazy and he was not a drunk. He was only about 10 years old — about my own age. He was wiry, strong and a great athlete.

It didn't cross my mind back then, but in recent years I have often wondered about the fate of Alex, his sister Lilia and his brother Leon. Growing up being a dumb Polack had its challenges, but in small town Kuroki there were folks of varying ethnicity: Ukrainians, Germans, Swedes, Norwegians, Czechoslovaks, English, Irish and Scottish. We were a hamlet of just

150 people, but we were a veritable United Nations. All of us were dumb once in a while, but it seemed the common racial prejudice of most folks was the "lazy Indian".

It is sad. From the white man the Indians received small pox, measles, tuberculosis and a variety of other exotic diseases. Then they got Indian Reservations and treaties which isolate them and make them second class citizens. They learned to abuse alcohol and gambling on countless Reservations where drug abuse and high suicide rates are rampant. They suffer from obesity, diabetes and heart disease from eating the fats and sugars we all love. Things don't seem to be working out for them. And everyone is surprised and shocked. We've given them so much and they're not grateful. They want more handed to them. They are just lazy Indians!

First Nations people are special, but every human being is special. If you take any humans, isolating them on reserves giving them little hope for the future you can expect suicide, drugs, prostitution, murder and dysfunction. Change is needed. Unfortunately the people in charge may have a vested interest in maintaining the status quo.

This is one person's opinion! But what do I know? I'm just a dumb Polack.

Sorry! I think I was barking again. For a few minutes I must have been absent-mindedly trying to save the world or maybe I morphed into a Rick Mercer clone, trying to imitate his rant. I have great respect for those First Nations individuals who have had the determination, common sense and will power to overcome all that is against them and be successful, but I wanted to draw attention to the needs of the forgotten. I did it my way!

*DesGeorges is not the real name. The story is true, but the names of the First Nations individuals have been changed to protect their privacy.

Hair Raising Experience

Life is an endless struggle full of frustrations and challenges, but eventually you find a hair stylist you like.

When we are in our youth, particularly in our teen years, we tend to be self-conscious about matters which may seem trivial to adults. The problems of racism, poverty, alcoholism, accidents, serious disease and abuse are monstrous compared to some of the minor issues we experienced as children. I have one problem which I try to take lightly, but it has been an issue for me from my very early Kuroki days. Many people in this world have much bigger problems and would just love to trade their problems for the little one I have.

All my life I have envied those with naturally beautiful hair and those with no hair at all. I apologize to the barbering and hairdressing professionals of North America. I have not had a haircut from a professional since 1973. I do not even know the current cost of a haircut for an average male. I have had unpleasant experiences with barbers. It's not their fault. For me there is no such thing as a bad hair day. I have had a bad hair **life**. I don't know if it's the shape of my head, the quality of my hair or my genetic makeup. But from my earliest remembrances my hair has been not unlike that of Dagwood in the Blondie comic strip.

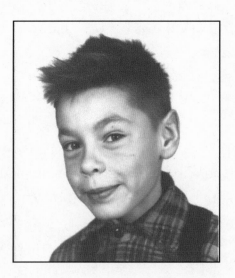

That's me – and that's my beautiful hair.

During the war my Dad learned the art of barbering, gave haircuts to some of his fellow soldiers and continued by cutting my hair and that of my male siblings in our younger days. However, his old set of manual clippers occasionally pinched and pulled hair out rather than cutting it, so we complained loudly whenever it was time for a trim. Dad did his best, but my unruly locks could not be tamed. My hair was such a mess that in the summer of 1952 when Uncle Nick - the dentist and bomb aimer from a previous chapter - came to Kuroki for a summer holiday, he told me and my dad the solution to my hair problem was a brush cut. With much complaining from me, getting out the scissors and clippers, he went to work on my head. Needless to say, he was a much better pilot and dentist than a barber, so the result was quite a disaster.

Kuroki's population would not support a full-time barber or hairdresser, but there was one resident, Art Pengally, who was a skilled barber, even possessing a genuine barber's chair. He did a part-time barbering business out of one corner of his living room, providing an excellent service to area residents. When I reached my teen years Dad sent me to him for a more professional cut; however, like others who worked on my head, he was fighting a losing battle.

Over the decades I have tried everything to try to control my unruly hair. During the late 1950's and early 1960's, my teenage years, life was especially traumatic. My hair was everywhere just at the age when I needed to look my best for those pretty things of the fairer sex who were attracting my attention. I wanted a hair style like Elvis Presley or James Dean who were the idols of all the teen girls. The duck tail hairstyle, otherwise known as duck butt, was the rage back then. It involved using great gobs of grease and fancy combing techniques to form the appearance of a duck's tail on the back of the head. I tried to imitate it, but my hair would not cooperate. Just when I thought all was lost I heard a snappy little jingle, and I was introduced to a marvelous new product.

> *Brycreem, a little dab will do you.*
> *Brylcreem, you'll look so debonair.*
> *Brylcreem, a little dab will do you.*
> *Simply rub a little in your hair.*

The only problem for me was that a little dab didn't do me! And I didn't look debonair. I used handfuls of the stuff, I was like a greased pig and it still wouldn't hold my hair down.

Until about 1973 I tried all varieties of greasy kid stuff available: Vitalis for beautiful hair, a variety of hair sprays and hair gels, and every hair care product imaginable as well as a product called mucilage, a type of glue all public school students used in the 1950's. All efforts were futile. In desperation I resorted to automotive products - axle grease, WD-40 and W5-30 motor oil. Needless to say, I was good for 3 months or 5000 miles, but my hair still looked like a rat's nest. Nothing worked! And some of the side effects were gruesome to behold.

In 1971 and 1972 I frequented a barbershop, which for lack of a better name and to avoid potential defamation lawsuits, I will refer to as the Barber and the Butcher. It was a father-son operation. The father, the Barber, who had dozens of years of experience cutting hair, was congenial and professional in his work. With what I gave him to work with, he performed miracles on my head of hair. His son, the one I refer to as the Butcher, must have taken his barbering training at the local hog slaughtering plant.

Unfortunately, almost every time I entered their shop, the Barber was busily cutting someone else's hair and there sat his son, the Butcher, reading a magazine and looking forlorn. Invariably, I didn't have the heart to wait for the Barber while letting the Butcher sit idle. I suffered the consequences. When I returned home after my episode at the guillotine Cecilia would look me over, sit me down in a chair and do her best to correct the handiwork of the Butcher. This routine became tiresome. I continued to look for alternatives.

One smartass co-worker with a handsome head of hair thought he was being helpful by suggesting that I try his barber, a high-class hair stylist who specialized in expensive razor cuts. I was reaching the end of my rope. I had to try something, so the next time I needed a haircut I booked an appointment with *the stylist* for a Saturday morning hair cut. It was a production to behold. First he looked over my head of hair assessing the task before him. He was impressive and professional. Next he **shampooed** my hair. **Shampooed!** Since I was a little child and my mother washed my hair I had never had my hair shampooed by a barber ever in my life. In fact no one had ever shampooed my hair for me. I had always done it for myself.

After the shampoo I was to experience the razor cut. This sculptor-artist-hairdresser-barber-stylist proceeded to strop his straight razor on the leather honing belt attached to the barber chair. Then with a flourish like the conductor of a symphony orchestra he wielded the instruments of his trade, occasionally stepping back to view the big picture. After what seemed like an eternity he handed me a mirror indicating that he was finished. It looked reasonably passable as it was still somewhat damp, holding the shape into which he had sculpted it. Then he took out his nuclear powered blow dryer, and brushing and blowing he futilely attempted to keep it in place. Next he donned his gas mask, took out a can of heavy duty hairspray and proceeded to use two cans of the sticky stuff before he again showed me the mirror. At that point I became rather suspicious, but when he again held the mirror to my face I thought the finished product looked rather attractive.

On my drive home I kept admiring myself in the rear view mirror until I attempted to stroke my beautiful head of hair. It felt like a vintage World War II helmet, perfectly shaped and unyielding. After a five-minute drive I was home to show Cecilia what the barber hath wrought. I hoped she would like it. At least there was the off chance that she wouldn't have to even it up as she had done when I returned from the handiwork of the Butcher. After we both assessed the situation, agreeing that it looked reasonably acceptable, I was still somewhat leery of what would happen when I shampooed out all the hairspray. I wanted to see if this fellow was truly a miracle worker, a charlatan or just good with a can of hairspray. The suspense was unbearable, but it needn't have been. My worst fears had materialized. The razor cut had been too short, and my hair stuck out in every direction. It was evenly cut, but it was too short for Cecilia to try to make improvements.

I was utterly depressed and miserable. My head was a mess, and there was no place I could hide. My options were extremely limited. I could shave my head, wear a hat for five or six weeks or commit suicide. The only consolation was that there did not appear in the vicinity to be any male hedgehogs who might try to mate with my head. That was the first and last time I darkened the door of that hair stylist.

Shortly after this most recent hair raising episode a savior appeared in the form of Jim, my younger brother. Jim is blessed with genetic disposition to follicular issues similar to mine, and in his search for an answer to tame his unruly mop he decided to try a perm. When I first heard of it I was somewhat skeptical because "perms are only for girls", but when I saw how good it looked on him I got the courage to try one in the privacy of my own home with Cecilia being the hair stylist and me being the very nervous patron doing all the back seat driving as she navigated my stubborn head of hair. She still recalls how the first few home perms were really difficult to administer because my very straight wiry mop wanted to pop out of the curlers. But after the first couple of sessions, when we very nearly had a trial separation over the home perm procedures, my hair started to become trained to fit into the curlers. Thereafter, we settled into a routine where every two months or so Cecilia would be my hairdresser, giving me a perm and a haircut and making me as beautiful as I am today.

After receiving that first perm I was somewhat self-conscious, but some of my friends and coworkers noticed a difference in my hair, and some even commented on how good it looked. I abashedly admitted that I was doing the girlie thing and experimenting with perms to tame my hair. The most amazing part of this whole experience was that for the first time in my life I didn't need to use any of the stinky, greasy, oily hair care products I had been addicted to for most of my life. I was becoming spoiled by the experience of having wash an' wear hair. Then, after a few months, when I met people or formed new friendships and met new acquaintances I would often receive comments about how lucky I was to have such nice natural curls in my hair. Sometimes I told them the truth. Sometimes I just thanked them for the compliment. Life was great!

My days, months and years of relatively uneventful hair experiences continued until 1991. In that year, Cecilia and I enjoyed an extended holiday to the Atlantic Provinces and Eastern United States during late August, all of September and early October. We were staying in campgrounds in a small fifth wheel travel trailer. During about the fifth week of our holiday in late September it became time for my routine perm to take place. We had prepared for this by bringing the perm solution and the curlers with us. At that time we were touring the state of Maine and ended up camping near a geological anomaly called the Desert of Maine. That evening we hiked in the sand dunes, enjoying the unusual scenery. We had decided that the next morning I would get my perm.

One can only imagine the satanic rituals performed by ancient peoples and inebriated teenagers in these mysterious dunes over the many millennia of their existence. It was time for us to make our own contribution to these strange practices. No one but our embarrassed son, Greg had ever witnessed the ritual of yours truly getting curlers and perm solution administered to his scalp and then sitting under a hair dryer to set the perm. The whole event was a very private matter, not for public viewing.

It was a cloudy, cool, late September morning. The campground was relatively deserted, and we would have liked to do the perm outside but the temperature was too cool, so Cecilia curled my hair and applied the perm solution while we were inside the fifth wheeler. When it was time to rinse out the perm solution we had to go outside because the trailer was too small to allow getting the task done without making a huge mess. I took my shirt off to avoid getting it soaking wet, and out we went.

Just then a family of five, two parents and three elementary school age children entered the adjacent campsite and started setting up camp. There I stood, shirt off, hair in curlers looking strange indeed. Cecilia followed me out with the rinse water and commenced the rinse. Suddenly the family looked at the weird scene confronting them and hastily repacked all their belongings and high tailed it out of there. Who knows what their motivation? But Cecilia and I speculated on it and giggled about it for days. We surmised that the family thought they were witnessing a lesbian couple in action. There was little tolerance for the gay and lesbian scene in 1991. Ellen DeGeneres didn't come out until 1997, and we suspected that the young family of campers didn't want to subject their little children to the utter depravity of seeing lesbians doing one another's hair. Or perhaps the horror of seeing the ugly, flat breasted, bare-chested lesbian getting her hair rinsed was just too much for them. Whatever the reason, we enjoyed several days of hilarity recalling the speedy departure of that innocent family and guessing what they were thinking and saying about the events that they had witnessed.

We still love telling friends and family about our experiences in the Desert of Maine, and even today Cecilia is my barber. However, in 1999 the ritual of the perm gave way to a simpler and more convenient buzz cut. I don't look as pretty as I did with the natural looking curls, but the routine is much faster and more carefree.

Cecilia asserts that I owe her about half a million dollars for services rendered. Good barbers and hairdressers cost money. She has provided me with the services of hairdresser-barber since about 1972. Add it up. That's over forty years, and for those services I am truly grateful, but half a million bucks is highway robbery. By my calculation the hairdressing services she provided from 1973 until 2014 amount to a debt of $16,800. That accounts for approximately eight salon treatments per year (either a perm or a haircut or both) for forty-two years at an estimated cost of $50 per treatment. I think that's fair and I will pay that to her. However, while we have the auditors in to balance the books perhaps we should settle other accounts. I occasionally mow the lawn and open stuck pickle jar lids. Those tasks should be worth something.

Making a Difference

Your talent is God's gift to you.
What you do with it is your gift
back to God. - Leo Buscaglia

Alicia, when I was a kid in Kuroki and even into my later life I was very frustrated by my hair, but I have learned to accept myself and my hair.

Besides, over the past fifty years Cecilia and I have had some real chuckles over various situations relating to my unmanageable locks. In the final analysis, beautiful hair, great collectibles, fancy cars, gobs of money and stunning good looks do not make a difference. The cost of haircuts, the amount I owe Cecilia or any calculation of credits and debits really are only a small part of life – they do not make a difference.

At the end of our life we cannot take our good looks, money, our antiques and our fancy toys with us. We go empty-handed. So, what is important; what does make a difference?

As I ponder all the characters I encountered in all of my "Kuroki's", I ask myself, **"What and who made the difference?"**

During my boyhood in Kuroki there was an old, grizzled alcoholic gentleman who always had time for the boys. We called him Old Man Peters* - Peters was his family name. He allowed us to sell his beer bottles. Then he used the proceeds to buy some tobacco which he shared with the boys who smoked. On one occasion, in the fall of 1954 during the autumn harvest he invited a group of half a dozen of us teen and pre-teen boys to go for a hike a short distance from town to watch the grain being harvested. There were teams of horses pulling wagons and men piling golden stooks of grain onto the wagons to take to the threshing machine which spewed straw and dust and bushels of golden wheat as it gobbled up the stooks. A few hundred yards from the threshing machine we sat on the stubble in a circle among the stooks watching history unfold, but we didn't understand the significance of the scene. Old Man Peters, squatting among us, sucking on an old corncob pipe and stroking his nicotine stained grey moustache, pointed out that this might be the last time we would see a scene like this. Horses were giving way to tractors and threshing machines were being replaced by combines. It took an old, unshaven alcoholic to spend time with us, to show us a piece of history in the making.

Back in Kuroki there was another man. He lived next door to us. I called him John McReady* in the story about the fellow who discovered gold while digging his toilet hole. He was a gentleman, often wearing a hat as he strolled down the street carrying a cane and tipping his hat to everyone he met on the street. He was a unique individual in so many ways. He entertained the youth of our hamlet by telling stories, singing songs and "blowing out his teeth". Having false teeth, he awed us six and seven year olds by rapidly expelling air through his throat, forcing his teeth part way out of his mouth. We loved it! At parties, anniversaries, amateur entertainment nights and socials he would always entertain the crowd with a song. But before he started singing, to the delight of the audience, he would remove his teeth and place them on top of the piano. In the days before television he helped create amazing, amusing local entertainment.

There was another man in Kuroki back in the 1950's. He was a younger man, about thirty-five years of age, holding down two jobs to support his growing family, not really having much spare time, but when he did he spent it with people. Like John McReady, he too loved to sing and dance and entertain at local social events. An amateur magician, he gave impromptu performances which wowed groups of children after school and on Saturdays, as well as entertaining adults at house parties and amateur shows. He loved being with people, giving people things, playing cards, telling jokes and treating people to food and to drink. He always showed hospitality. Everyone who ever came to his home was treated to food and drink. People staying overnight with him were always awakened to the smell of bacon frying, coffee brewing, a hearty "Good-morning" and a shot of Lemon Gin or Orange Gin, so that they didn't miss out on their morning vitamin C. Incomparable hospitality!

This man also gave me advice – frequently! He wanted me to learn and profit from his experience, not to suffer through the same mistakes that he did. However, it was not my job to follow advice. For the most part I listened, sometimes impatiently, to his counsel and guidance; then I went my own way to make my own mistakes, to live my own life. The man I speak of here is Mike Sliva, my Dad. As I am writing these words, on December 21, 2014 my Father is passing from this world to the next. He is experiencing one of life's greatest mysteries – death, which we all wonder about, and fear, but which every human being encounters. I wish him an awesome voyage!

My Dad experienced a life longer than most people, ninety-five years plus forty-seven days. His granddaughter, (that's you, Alicia) experienced only forty hours. In reflecting upon life I have to wonder why one person gets forty hours of life and another gets ninety-five years. I know there is a plan, and one day it may be revealed to us. Dad loved all his children, grandchildren and great grandchildren, and I know he would have gladly given some of his years to you, Alicia, but it was not to be. We cannot give our life; we can only share it with those around us and my Dad did so.

So, in life, what is important? What makes a difference? Could it be that being a friend and sharing unselfishly make the biggest difference?

* **Not the real family names. The names have been changed to protect family privacy.**

Our New Kuroki

To every man is given a key to the gates of heaven. The same key opens the gates of hell. - Buddhist Proverb

We knew we couldn't stay in our "Kuroki" forever. We hung on as long as we could, but eventually we knew we would have to leave. My Dad died on December 21, 2014. He couldn't wait until the anniversary of my Mother's death – December 22, 1995. He arrived there a day early! What a guy! He has probably already ordered a photographer and they are taking anniversary portraits –Alicia, maybe you are in the photo!

As we age we sometimes contemplate our own endings – and new beginnings. We get a changing perspective of life and death. Assuming we are in good health we might like to live a life span of one hundred years. We aren't satisfied with the eighty years God gave us in the little story about the creation of life – we want to hang on a little longer. So, one hundred years might not be unreasonable given the improvements to health care and technological assists to our physical and mental well-being. If, like me, you are over fifty years of age, the countdown to one hundred has begun. Life might be closer to ending and death might be closer to beginning. We would be lying if we didn't admit that we ask questions more often about what happens after we kick the proverbial bucket. Does our existence cease? If we continue to exist, what form do we take? Is there heaven? Is there hell? What are they like? Will we meet God face to face? Will we understand, at least a little bit, the mysteries of the universe? Will we truly have no more troubles and no more tears? Will it be everlasting? Everlasting is a long time. Will we get tired and bored with "forever"?

For the answers to these and many other questions related to the afterlife and what lies in store for us after death you may want to consult your Bible, your Koran, your Torah or other holy books. I do not have answers, but here I'd like to share some thoughts that you might not find in any of the holy books.

Some folks have difficulty believing there is an afterlife and that it is everlasting or infinite. I have no problem with it at all. In fact I find it difficult to imagine otherwise. Can anything ever be infinite? Well, yes! Take our universe for example. Scientists tell us it doesn't end and common sense tells us that you can't reach the end of our universe. You don't come to a brick wall or a fence with a big poster or flashing neon sign saying, "You have come to the edge of the universe. There is nothing on the other side of this barrier."

So, if our universe goes on and on and on and on forever, is it possible that we might do the same?

And if we are to believe some of the teachings of Jesus, the afterlife can be filled with wonder and awe and marvels. If so, what awaits us? I like to believe that what awaits us is very different for each of us. As humans, we have similarities, but we are created to be individuals. We all have our individual likes, dislikes, preferences and loves. Our opinions as to what is an ideal Heaven - our "New Kuroki" - can be as varied as our preferences regarding an ideal temperature, the saltiness or spiciness of our food, our desire for solitude or companionship, our preference for comedy or tragedy, our love or abhorrence of jazz, blues, rock 'n roll, rap, easy listening, big band, country music or bluegrass. If God is truly a God of love, and I believe He is, Heaven will be big and open and loving enough to accommodate the quirks, preferences and desires of everyone worthy to enter and remain there.

Our New Kuroki will be something like a band playing a wondrous, beautiful, marvelous melody with each of us hearing only the genre and instruments and vocals and rhythm that appeal most to our senses, or if we just want peace and quiet we might hear absolutely nothing. It will be something like eating in an unbeliev-able banquet hall where the menu is infinitely varied to appeal to each individual's taste buds. And the wine never tasted so good. It all comes from the same carafe, but it tastes amazing to everyone. We drink all we like, we are always happy, but we are never obnoxious, drunk or hung over. Or maybe it won't be like that at all for you. Maybe you don't care for music or fine food and wine. Maybe you like to eat in solitude and enjoy a big juicy loaded hamburger, with onion rings, fries and root beer without concerning yourself about the salt, fat, sugar and cholesterol content of what you are consuming. Do you think God can accommodate that? You can bet your big belly on that one.

What is Heaven for me? Well, I enjoy challenges. Maybe it's the realization that when I am challenged I know that the result will not be perfection, but that success or achievement is all relative and that even if there is no perfection maybe I can keep improv-ing. I am finding that writing a book is like that. Relationships are often like that. Marriage is like that. Life is like that. And certainly GOLF is like that. So, after the music and dancing and fine dining, is Heaven one big challenging golf course? I like to think so. But maybe golf isn't your cup of tea. Lest I hear mumbling and grumbling about my vision of Heaven from the non-golfers, remember that in God's Heaven you get to create your own piece of Paradise - your own Kuroki. Maybe your vision includes chess, poetry, football or skating or horseback riding. Go for it!

On our journey through life - and all of our Kuroki's - all humans have trials, problems, hopes and fears. However, if we concentrate on the struggles in our lives we are missing out on all the sweetness, the real fun to be experienced, the family things. As the song goes, "We - are - family". We are all brethren and "sistern" as one comedian put it. Sometimes we just don't act like we are.

In the end we are all the same; we are equal. Prince Harry is equal to my golfing buddy, Moe, who is equal to Albert Einstein, who is equal to my brother Don, who is equal to Tiger Woods, who is equal to my sister, Margaret, who is equal to Queen Elizabeth who is equal to the helpless, hopeless, homeless alcoholic spending the night in some dirty back alley. There are no Dumb Polacks, no Lazy Indians. We are the same and we are equal.

It is said that a picture paints a thousand words. In the middle ages some European stone masons were philosophers and deep thinkers. They left messages in their carvings on the exterior walls of some of the buildings on which they worked. In this stone carving the stone mason asks us, "Which person is the king and which is the subject?"

In the democracy of the dead all men at last are equal. There is neither rank nor station nor prerogative in the republic of the grave. - John James Ingalls

Epilogue

The reason it hurts so much to separate is because our souls are connected. Maybe they always have been and will be. - Nicholas Sparks, The Notebook

My Dear Alicia,

Thank you for asking me to take this little journey with you, for asking me to tell you about life. When we started we didn't know where it would lead us. We don't often like to talk about it or to think about it, but life is intertwined with death. And you know more about that than I do, since you have experienced death, and I have yet to go down that path.

I have not only told you the story of some of my life, but also some of my philosophy of life. This story has no ending; it goes on forever. We are all part of the music of the cosmos, the heavens and the stars – part of God's song, which is a never ending song – the song of creation which goes on forever. However, this book is ending (except for the great recipes, the credits, the sincere acknowledgements and the invitation to my readers).

Good night and farewell, Alicia, until we meet again.

We will meet again!

Love,

Daddy

Good Night

Whispering, wondering,
Awe in the night;
Gazing, praising,
God's great delight;
Shimmering, glimmering,
Stars shining bright;
Under the glow of the sky filled with light,
With gentleness, God's breath,
Calming our fright;
All through the universe drifting along,
God's whole creation becomes His song.

By night, an atheist half believes in God.
- Edward Young, Night Thoughts

Part Three

Recipes

If God had intended us to follow recipes, He wouldn't have given us grandmothers. - Linda Henley

I want to make it easy to prepare good food, so the recipes I'm including in the next few pages are time-saving, easy to prepare and delicious. They are all based on traditional Polish-Ukrainian ethnic recipes like my Granny prepared. She prepared some awesome traditional foods. The recipes which follow aren't her recipes, but they are based on foods we really enjoyed when we were growing up and which we prepare and eat frequently to this day. Most important, these are primarily vegetarian recipes and very nutritious. The one exception to the "easy to prepare" criteria is this first one for borscht, but when you try it you will find it is well worth the extra time and energy.

Cheap Like Borscht

It's better to have no spoon than to have no soup. - German Proverb

On the prairies we have a saying, "Cheap like borscht".

Yes, borscht is cheap if you are willing to spend backbreaking time and energy planting, watering and weeding a big garden to eventually harvest the fruits of your labour. Yes, it's cheap if you are willing to care for, shelter, feed and milk a cow and to separate the milk to get thick, rich, fresh cream. If you regard your time and labour as having no value the borscht will be almost free. And it will be delicious. There is really no other food like it. Borscht made from fresh home grown ingredients will make you think you have died and gone to a very nice place. I suggest growing a small garden and having at least some fresh ingredients. You will fall in love all over again.

However, if you have neither the time nor the inclination to do some vegetable gardening your borscht can still be delicious. The bad news is that it is not free; it is now moderately priced as far as soup goes, but it is still delicious.

One of my favorite foods is borscht. Many borscht recipes have been handed down from generation to generation in most Polish and Ukrainian families with slight modifications from time to time to suit individual's tastes. This specific recipe is a vegetarian family favorite which was used by Cecilia's mother and is used by Cecilia to this day. At the end of the recipe there are variations which include broth and meat options.

Before you start, here is your shopping list:

⊗ 2 cups of finely chopped cabbage

⊗ one heaping tablespoon of butter

⊗ 3 cups of tomato juice

⊗ one stick finely chopped celery

⊗ one carrot diced

⊗ one large potato cut into small cubes

⊗ one large cooking onion diced

- ⊗ two beets about the size of oranges, diced

- ⊗ two heaping tablespoons chopped fresh dill

- ⊗ one 19 ounce can of Navy or Romano beans

- ⊗ some whipping cream

- ⊗ salt and pepper to taste

For this recipe you will need two cooking pots, a small one which can hold about 6 cups of liquid and one large soup pot or Dutch oven which can hold about 20 to 25 cups of liquid.

Into the smaller pot place the following ingredients:

- ⊗ 2 cups of finely chopped cabbage

- ⊗ one heaping tablespoon of butter

- ⊗ 1 teaspoon of salt

- ⊗ 3 cups of tomato juice and half cup of water

Bring these ingredients to a boil then turn the heat to simmer while you prepare the other ingredients. Cabbage takes longer to cook than the other ingredients so it will be ready by the time the large pot of ingredients have cooked. While the cabbage and tomato mixture is simmering prepare the ingredients for the large pot as follows:

- ⊗ 10 cups water

- ⊗ one stick finely chopped celery

- ⊗ one carrot diced

- ⊗ one large potato cut into small cubes

- ⊗ one large cooking onion diced

- ⊗ two beets about the size of oranges, diced

- ⊗ one heaping teaspoon salt

- ⊗ two heaping tablespoons chopped fresh dill

Bring the large pot to a boil, then reduce the heat to simmer. Simmer the large pot of ingredients covered for about 25 minutes or until the vegetables are cooked and tender. Then add the 19 ounce or 540 mL can of Navy or Romano beans as well as the cooked tomato and cabbage mixture. Simmer all of these ingredients together for about 10 minutes to blend the flavors.

In a cup, mix about ¼ cup of whipping cream with about one heaping tablespoon of flour. Blend well; then stir the whipping cream-flour mixture into the borscht in the large pot. Extra cream may be added for extra richness if desired. Small lumps of flour will eventually dissolve. Serve and enjoy.

Variations (try one or more of the following):

⊗ 1 L of chicken or beef broth may be
substituted for some of the water

⊗ add a small ham bone to the large
pot while it is simmering

⊗ instead of using whipping cream, a dollop of sour
cream may be put into each bowl at serving time

⊗ Our own invention is Mexican borscht. Simply
add a tablespoon or two of your favorite salsa
to your own bowl of borscht just at meal time.

⊗ You may want salt, pepper and Tabasco
or other hot sauce on the table at serving
time to suit each individual taste

With time and experimentation you will vary the basic
ingredients slightly to suit your own tastes. This recipe
will serve about 10 people. We make it for two people
and have plenty of leftovers for a couple of weeks. Put
the extra in glass jars, cover, cool, then store in your
refrigerator for up to two weeks to use for a tasty snack
at any time. As with most soups, borscht always seems
to taste better the next day.

Doukhobor Borscht

Nothing would be more tiresome than eating and drinking if God had not made them a pleasure as well as a necessity. - Voltaire

This recipe for Russian style borscht is one of simplest, most delicious soup recipes in existence. Fondly named "Doukhoborski Borscht", inexpensive and hearty it is an old family favorite from Cecilia's family. We make it frequently, particularly in autumn when we have an abundance of over-ripe, fresh-from-the-garden tomatoes. It can be made using canned tomatoes, but the flavor of home-grown tomatoes is incomparable.

Ingredients:

⊗ 8 cups of water

⊗ 3 cups chopped over-ripe tomatoes (fresh or canned)

⊗ 2 cups finely chopped cabbage

⊗ ½ red or green bell pepper, finely chopped

⊗ 1 diced medium yellow cooking onion

⊗ 1 large potato diced

⊗ 1 tablespoon butter

⊗ 1 heaping teaspoon salt (more or less depending upon whether you are using fresh garden tomatoes or already salted canned tomatoes)

⊗ Salt and pepper to taste at serving time

⊗ Simply put all the ingredients into a soup pot and bring to a boil. Reduce heat to low, cover and simmer for 30 minutes.

Enjoy!

Lazy Cabbage Rolls

*Where love sets the table, the food
tastes best. - French Proverb*

Granny never made these. There was nothing lazy
about her cabbage rolls. She slaved long hours in the
garden growing cabbages, preserving them as sauerkraut and whole heads of sour cabbage in the autumn;
then when she made cabbage rolls she made the filling,
lovingly individually hand-wrapping each tiny delicious
cabbage roll. These two recipes are as good, but they
are much simpler to prepare and just as nutritious.
The traditional Polish cabbage roll is made with a
buckwheat filling. Having a nuttier taste and utilizing
sauerkraut it is our preference for special feasts like
Easter or Christmas, but for people not familiar with
the buckwheat-sauerkraut flavor it may be too daunting

for the palate. The fresh cabbage and rice recipe is a milder flavor and very simple to make.

Buckwheat – Sauerkraut Lazy Cabbage Rolls
Ingredients:

⊗ 1 cup of whole buckwheat

⊗ 1 jar of sauerkraut – we have tried many brands as well as homemade sauerkraut. Our hands down favorite is the least expensive and absolute tastiest. It is the one litre jar of Loblaws yellow label "No Name" Wine Sauerkraut in a clear glass jar.

⊗ 1 large yellow onion, minced

⊗ 1 tablespoon butter

⊗ Salt and pepper to taste – not much salt is needed as the sauerkraut is quite salty.

Method:

Use two cooking pots. In the first pot cook the whole buckwheat as directed on the package instructions. In the second pot on medium heat sauté the minced onion in one tablespoon of butter.

While the buckwheat and onions are cooking drain and rinse the sauerkraut. When the buckwheat and onions are ready mix them together with the sauerkraut, a few generous shakes of pepper and a little salt. Place the mixture in a large greased casserole dish, covered, into a 325 degree preheated oven for about

45 minutes. My personal preference is to overcook this dish a little, caramelizing the edges slightly for a nuttier taste.

This dish as well as the fresh cabbage lazy cabbage roll recipe which follows is an excellent substitute for potatoes. The baking duration is not critical giving you time for preparing other things or visiting with guests. If after an hour you are still not ready to eat just check the casserole; if it looks a little dry add one half cup of water, replace the lid and lower the temperature until you are ready to eat.

Fresh Cabbage and Rice Lazy Cabbage Rolls
Ingredients:

⊗ 1 cup of rice

⊗ 3 or 4 cups of cabbage, coarsely chopped

⊗ 1 large yellow onion, minced

⊗ 1 can condensed tomato soup (we prefer the flavor of generic)

⊗ 1 tablespoon butter

⊗ Salt and pepper to taste

Use one small frying pan and two cooking pots for the preparation. In the first pot cook the rice according to the package directions. In the second pot with one-quarter cup of water cook the cabbage with a few shakes of salt and pepper until it is just tender. In the frying pan sauté the minced onion in one tablespoon of butter.

When all three ingredients are cooked mix them all together with the can of condensed tomato soup, a little salt and some generous shakes of black pepper. Place the mixture in a large greased casserole dish, covered, into a preheated oven set at 325 degrees for forty-five minutes.

Enjoy!

Part Four

Appreciation
and Invitation

Photography/ Image Credits

Front Book Cover: Sleepy beagle dog in funny glasses near laptop - Photo courtesy of Bigstock.com, copyright by soloway.

Page 6 - Kuroki Billboard - Photo taken by author's cousin, Reverend Father Rudolph Nowakowski.

Page 27 - Old Wooden Outhouse - Photo courtesy of Bigstock. com, copyright by Karen VanDenBerge.

Page 74 - Lancaster Bomber and flight crew - Photo courtesy of author's Aunt, Helen Mazer.

Page 85 - Television Test Pattern –
Public use image from internet.

Page 92 - Café-Dining room in Kuroki hotel with author's youngest siblings: Margaret, Jim and John. Photo taken by author's father, Mike Sliva

Page 116 - Author's brother Jim aged 3, together with sister Margaret and friends - Photo taken by author's father, Mike Sliva.

Page 117 - Author's brother Jim aged 47, together
with the author, Brother John and Father Mike
Sliva. - Photo from author's collection.
Page 166 - Author's youngest brother,
John and his dog, Ginger - Photo taken
by author's father, Mike Sliva.
Page 202 - School photo of the author
from author's archives.
Page 224 - Stone carving on an old building in
Germany - Photo taken from author's collection.
Page 256 - Map of North America – courtesy
of Bigstock.com, copyright Bruce Jones.
Page 257 - Map of Kuroki area – by the author.

Acknowledgements

There comes a point in your life when you realize who really matters, who never did, and who always will.

I am much indebted to all who supported me during the rollercoaster ride of writing, editing and publication. I could not have accomplished this publication on my own. My super-ego tells me that everything I write is close to perfect, even though I know it's a lie. My reviewers, critics and editors have helped me to see things from a different perspective, to come down to earth. Good reviewers are like ultra-smooth plate glass mirrors reflecting a truer image of my handicraft. I know it is a difficult task to show someone that he has produced garbage, but then to encourage him to recycle it into something more attractive or utilitarian and in some cases to assign it to the garbage heap. My sincere thank you to everyone who helped me!

For their technical support, patience in dealing with a novice author, genuine helpfulness and courteous staff, Friesen's is second to none. The incisive editorial evaluation with specific suggestions for improvement as well as identification of strengths in my manuscript provided me with ideas to refine and reinforce my central themes. Thank you, staff of Friesen Press.

Thank you also to Bigstock.com for providing a tremendous service with thousands of excellent images on their website, a few of which I have used for my book, including the cover page.

To my wife Cecilia the first, the best and the most severe of my critics who kept asking me, "What is the point?" and to my son Greg who told me to focus and who kept asking me, "Do you want the book to be finished, or do you want the book to be good?", I thank you from the bottom of my heart. Greg, my discussions with you helped me to focus, giving me purpose for my narrative and helping me to see that sometimes "less is more". Cecilia and Greg more than anyone else encouraged, criticized and cajoled me to do better. I love and appreciate both of you.

Thank you to Robyn, my sixteen year old granddaughter, an avid reader who agreed to review my barking and to provide me with feedback from a teen perspective. I love you, Robyn.

Barbara, my dear sister, you were the first to suffer through the reading of a very early draft of my writings. Your honesty in providing me with verbal feedback, telling me which parts you didn't like caused me to rethink the whole direction of my barking; then you provided me with valuable edits in the later stages of my authoring journey. I love you and sincerely appreciate your help, forthrightness, encouragement and critical analysis.

Don and Joyce Nakrieko, you are long time good friends in so many ways. Thank you for your friendship and terrific sense of humour. Don, you were the first non-family member to read any of my writings, encouraging me to continue writing and enjoying good Scotch. Don and Joyce, after reading my semi-final draft manuscript, you both provided me with positive, encouraging commentary and made very helpful suggestions for improvement. You even speculated that I might write another book. Who knows? Thank you for your kindness and friendship.

Don Bodnarchuk, my friend, golfing buddy and fellow masochist in this wild, weird world of writing, I thank you for reading my draft manuscript and for making many valuable suggestions to improve its readability. My discussions with you spurred me on to complete my publishing journey.

Finally to my Mother who died many years ago, to my father who died just as I was completing a third rewrite of my book, and to all my brothers and sisters for agreeing to be the subjects of my ramblings, barking and nostalgic reminiscences, you were my first family. I cherish your love, value your friendship and thank you for all you have done and continue to do to maintain our family ties in spite of the miles and years which separate us.

Invitation to my Readers

Thank you for following my journey. It is my sincere hope that you enjoyed my barking and that you will share my reminiscences and stories with your friends and relatives. If you have any commentary or feedback for me I would be thrilled to receive an email from you at barkingfromthefrontporch@yahoo.com

As well, if you have any inclination to continue our journey together I invite you to visit my website at www.barkingfromthefrontporch.com. It is a work in progress, but I plan to have fun, fantasy, humor, information, political commentary and benevolence as well as deep thoughts about life and death included in more of my barking there. Several draft chapters which I originally intended for publication herein were not printed because of sage advice from my editors and critics who tried to keep me on a tight leash. Old dogs sometimes have Attention Deficit Disorder causing them to wander off looking for a car to chase or a fire hydrant on which to urinate. Just like Ginger in the chapter entitled *Puppy Love*, I sometimes yearn to just chase a few rabbits and do some barking. Some of that barking will likely be material for my website. In addition, for any aspiring authors I plan to share some of my novice writing, editing, re-writing and publishing experiences.

Most certainly I will have more information, photos and maybe even some more stories about my Kuroki. You are invited. Please join me. If you have an anecdote or a photo that you would like to share for posting on the website please feel free to send it to me by email attachment at barkingfromthefrontporch@yahoo.com

I cannot promise that I can include everything that is sent, but I will most certainly acknowledge your efforts and try to include it.

Peace be with you and yours.

Kuroki Area

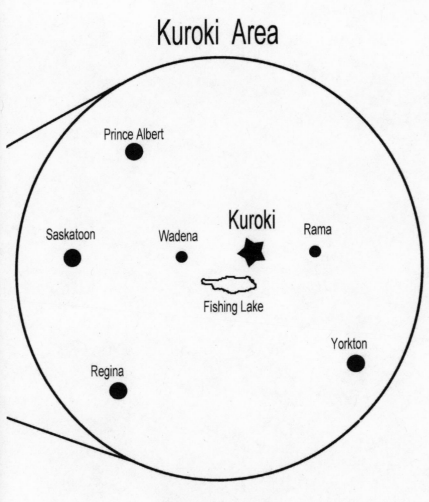

Prince Albert

Kuroki

Saskatoon   Wadena   Rama

Fishing Lake

Yorkton

Regina

Map not to scale

Printed in Canada